Get Out Of The "DRY PLACES!"

Vinson + Danella
Be Blessed, Indeed!

D. R. Williams

7/30/07

Other Books by the Author

Help to GET OVER IT!

When Circumstances Have Us Stuck and
Powerless to Move Forward

Get Out Of The "DRY PLACES!"

The Battle Belongs To GOD!

D. R. Williams

Copyright © 2007 by D. R. Williams.

ISBN: Hardcover   978-1-4257-2777-2
                  Softcover   978-1-4257-2776-5

All rights reserved. No part of this book may be reproduced or transmitted in any form or by any means, electronic or mechanical, including photocopying, recording, or by any information storage and retrieval system, without permission in writing from the copyright owner.

This book was printed in the United States of America.

To order additional copies of this book, contact:
Xlibris Corporation
1-888-795-4274
www.Xlibris.com
Orders@Xlibris.com
35927

CONTENTS

Acknowledgments 9
Foreword 11
Introduction 13

Praying Time

1. The Desert 25
2. The Lie 32
3. The Pain 42
4. The Fear 52

Press On

5. The Wait 63
6. The Servant/Leader 70
7. The Aged 79
8. The Pass Code 88

Praise Worthy

9. The Laughter 98
10. The Passion 107
11. The Peace 113
12. The Favor 119

About the Author 131

A variety of Bible versions were selected for clarification purposes. Although the Bible must never be mishandled by private interpretations, the author's insights can be obscured by failing to select the words that explain the points emphasized. I pray that each version selected add an element of personal revelation to the reader. Each version and abbreviations are listed below in the order they appear.

NKJV—New King James Version Copyright @ 1974, 1978, 1982, Thomas Nelson, Inc. Publishers

NIV—New International Version Copyright @ 1973, 1978, 1984, by International Bible Society

AMP—Scripture taken from the Amplified Bible, Old Testament copyright @ 1965, 1987 by the Zondervan Corporation. The Amplified new testament copyright @ 1958, 1987 by the Lockman Foundation. Used by permission.

Message—Message Translation Copyright @ 1993, 1994, 1995, 1996, 200, 2001, 2002. Used by permission of NavPress Publishing Group.

TLB—The Living Bible Copyright @ 1971 by Tyndale House Publishers, Wheaton, IL. Used by permission.

CEV—Contemporary English Version. Copyright @1995, American Bible Society

KJV—King James Version Copyright @ 1989 by World Publishing

NASB—New American Standard Bible Copyright @ 1960, 1962, 1963, 1968, 1971, 1972, 1973, 1975, 1977, the Lockman Foundation

Explanation of General Format

Proper Name of GOD—Out of deep reverence for the names of GOD, whenever mentioned in this book, all letters are capitalized.

Personal Pronouns—In every instance pertaining to Deity, all letters are capitalized.

Prayers—The prayers are communications directed to GOD therefore all references are made in the first person and letters are capitalized in bold print when pertaining to Deity.

In Dedication
To the thousands
Of men and women who
Serve their country in the
United States Armed Services.

Special recognition and gratitude
Goes to the soldiers
Who leave their families,
Loved ones and country
To labor over seas in
The combat zones.

Holy Scripture urges each believer

To endure hardship like a

First-class soldier of JESUS CHRIST

Because no soldier in service

Becomes entangled in the enterprises

Of civilian life; his or her aim

Is to satisfy and please the

One who enlisted him.

ACKNOWLEDGMENTS

Special Thanks to my Husband John, who is my soul mate and ministry partner. You have been my love and by my side for over three decades; from college sweetheart, parenting five children together, while I served on the clergy staff at several churches and now in my efforts to spread the good news of JESUS CHRIST as an author and inspirational coach. Your quiet and steady support has been a constant that I can depend on.

Thanks to my Mother and prayer partner, Rosa B. Freeman. You are a great source of inspiration and encouragement. You read my manuscript in the rough draft stages and helped to edit for corrections. As a proud Christian mother, you organized book signings, purchased books for gifts and helped to fund author presentations.

Thanks to my Big Brother Joseph A. Baker and sister-in-law Juanita who sponsored the publication of this second book in the HELP! Series. Your tangible support caused this project to move from the realm of what could be to what now is!

Thanks to my children, Keisha, Anita, Emojoy, John II and Dana who always cheer on my projects. Your questions and observations serve as the relevance check for me to Keep It Real! *(KIR)*

Thanks to my sons-in-law; Omari Moore and A.J. Brown, you both have made my daughters happy and offered encouragement for my writing projects. Thanks to my brand new daughter-in-law, Candace. You have loved my son through his last years at West Point and now serve as a military wife whose spouse is deployed to combat zones. Keep the Faith!

Special thanks to my "Nana Babies"; Christian James, Camille Diana and Kayla Renee. You each show forth the Blessings of Abraham. It is a joy being your Nana!

Thanks to my siblings; Vinson, Emogene and Chris and my in-laws; Danella, LaMont, Cheryl, A.J., Annabel, Katie, Adolphus, Elliot Jr., James, Monica, Joseph, Charles, Velma, Louis, Earl, Anthony, My Uncle Zeb Langston, Jr. and Aunt Mabel as well as other family members for your love and support. May this book also be a blessing for you.

Thanks to Mary Clendeninn, my good friend since high school. You have also read the rough draft manuscript and offered editorial suggestions.

GOD promises not to leave us comfortless so there are many special people that HE sends in our lives to help us. Thank you to the ministers, sponsors, supporters, editors and dear friends who purposed to get this project into the hands of the public. Thank you for those joining me in prayer for favor with this book in advertisement and distribution. Thank you to every reading ministry, book club and study group who selects this book for discussion. Thank you to the Churches, Christian Book stores, and Christian Library who obtain this book as a part of your inventory. May GOD richly Bless you indeed! May your life never be the same from this point forward and may you continue to thrive in sweet communion with GOD, Almighty!

FOREWORD

Dear Readers,

Over the years, it has been a part of my ministry assignment to intercede in prayer for others. My assignment has included praying for leadership, people in ministry, those in trouble and most recently whenever disaster strikes.

Every time I hear of catastrophe and tragedies or when facing any major task, I am compelled to travail in prayer. Several years ago, my assignment expanded to include writing prayers and making them available that others might bind their heart together with me in a united petition to the LORD. I began to write Bible studies, devotions, articles and most recently books to inspire others to run whole-heartedly to GOD.

Early Sunday, September 25, 2005 at 3:30 a.m., I awoke to receive a powerful and comforting word from the LORD. I got up and wrote word for word what I heard. I have included that word in this book as a platform to call people everywhere to prayer at all times. Get closer to GOD and HE will get closer to you. Meditate on HIS word daily. Open your heart to receive HIS promises. Be encouraged as you read the prophetic word GOD has sent to harvest HIS abundant blessings in your life. Rejoice in HIS generosity and never forget how lavishly GOD loves you. Be Blessed, Indeed!

Rev. D.R. Williams

"Tell MY people not to loose heart or become faint. I am perfecting those things, which concerns you. You are entering into a new season. I am rebuilding you. I am remaking you. I am refreshing you.

Don't become stuck on what has happened in the past. Yesterday is gone and I will help you to get over it. I will not leave you bereft. I will turn your sorrow into laughter. I will give you joy unspeakable. Your weeping during the night has ended. You are standing on the dawn of a new day.

Take courage, keep moving forward. Worship ME with a sincere heart. Don't forget how much I love you. You are MY Beloved. I will take you to heights you've never seen before. I will bless you like never before. Your joy in ME will be complete.

I see you. I hear your prayers, I know when you cry. I will now move to make things right for you. You have not run scared during these times of acute testing. Now I will reward you.

Give ME all of your burdens, cares and anxiety. I care for you and you no longer have to carry them. What the enemy meant to harm you and bring evil upon you, I have turned around for your good and will bless you abundantly.

Don't loose heart. Don't faint. I am with you," says the LORD.

INTRODUCTION

Are you growing everyday? Or, have you reached a point of regression? Sometimes life can really surprise you. Just when you may think you have it all figured out, life throws you a major curve ball. I can think of the image of a person skating merrily around and around a frozen lake, perhaps in a snowy meadow, a little before dusk. Maybe the skater is humming a sweet melody with arms out stretched adoring the wonders of nature. It is not too cold nor is it very windy. All outwardly appear to be a perfect time for enjoying nature. I can almost hear the laughter and satisfaction the skater expresses as each skating feat is accomplished effortlessly. Little does the unsuspecting skater know that he or she is skating on thin ice! Just a couple of more turns around the lake and the skater will break through to the dark, frigid and menacing water lurking beneath.

You and I may reach a point in life when we feel just like the skater. We may feel that we are dotting all of the I's and crossing all the T's in our lives. We may be merrily skating through life when suddenly out of nowhere it seems that the bottom has fallen out.

The skater who survives this ordeal does not pass Go, and does not collect $200.00, but is transported in a flash to one of life's "**DRY PLACES**". This seemingly unexpected or undeserved calamity could push any of us to the "**DRY PLACES**". We may begin to wonder how we misread all of the signs leading up to this catastrophe. Why did this happen? Oh, if only we could go back to the way it was.

Sometimes, it does not take horrible incidents for us to travel to the "**DRY PLACES**". It could be that while we are serving GOD and waiting for that allusive M-O-R-E, we may become stuck in the "**DRY PLACES**".

There is nothing attractive or appealing about the **"DRY PLACES"**, yet many become stuck there. Often the **"DRY PLACES"** appear so vast that we can be tempted to set up residence there, afraid that it is the best we can do! I chuckle as I remember when my daughter heard about this book project she said, "Even the Sahara Desert has an end!" In other words, we are not meant to stay in the **"DRY PLACES"** forever.

The word "DRY" leads us to words like; dehydrated, dried out, dried up, arid, waterless, desiccated, shriveled, shrunken, parched, thirsty, distressed, disappointed, let down, disheartened, obsolete, drought, shallow, inactive, having little moisture, barren, withered, over ripe, longing, yearning, hurting, wounded, upset and in a panic.

The **"DRY PLACES"** brings images of deserts, wastelands, rough country, harsh environments or a wilderness. It is a lonely place where nothing good is expected to happen. The psalmist cries out, *"O GOD, you are my GOD, earnestly I seek you; my soul thirsts for you, my body longs for you, in a dry and weary land where there is no water.* Psalm 63: 1 NIV

The Amplified Version puts it this way, *"O GOD, You are my GOD, earnestly will I seek You; my inner self thirsts for You, my flesh longs and is faint for You, in a dry and weary land where no water is."* Psalm 63:1-4 Amplified

What happens when you serve the LORD with all of your might and yet it appears that you have reached an impasse? How do you pick yourself up and go on? What if you are in a position of leadership and desire for someone to come alongside you and lift your spirits?

As one of the pastors of a large urban church, I came across many who have allowed problems and life challenges to drive them to the **"DRY PLACES"**. The **"DRY PLACES"** have held reservations for me from time to time. They have called and beckoned to me with sales pitches laced to wallow in pity, fatigue and frustration. The **"DRY PLACES"** promise that once you arrive you can stay without interruptions, misunderstandings and busy schedules. (They never mention that things like love, joy and peace are not there either!)

No, **"DRY PLACES"**, I have learned to avoid your trappings. The Message Translation puts it this way in that same passage in the sixty-third Psalm.

"GOD—you're my GOD! I cannot get enough of you! I've worked up such hunger and thirst for GOD, traveling across dry and weary deserts." In other words, GOD is the only thing that can satisfy. We look at the Bible for actual cases where it seemed that there was no way out for some in the **"DRY PLACES"**. Yet repeatedly we discovered that help was dispatched from GOD.

Let us go back and consider the skater in the analogy in the beginning of this chapter. We do not know why that skater was alone skating on thin ice. We could assign blame and think to ourselves that he or she should have known better. It was foolish on the part of the skater not to ensure that the frozen lake could handle his or her weight. No matter, assigning blame will not fix the situation or solve the problem. Instead, the skater needs the LORD!

GOD has given us this promise in HIS holy word. *"For HE shall give HIS angels charge over you, to keep you in all your ways. In their hands, they shall bear you up, lest you dash your foot against a stone.* Psalm 91:11-12 NKJV. This means we must not cast away our confidence in GOD'S ability to take good care of us.

For the journey through the **"DRY PLACES"**, we must be led by GOD'S HOLY SPIRIT. The prophet Joel wrote that in the last days, GOD would pour out HIS Sprit upon all flesh. The HOLY SPIRIT will then endow us all with power from on high that will sustain us even in the driest of times. GOD'S HOLY SPIRIT will help us to *Grow* through rather than to simply *Go* through the **"DRY PLACES."** Grow is a verb that describes an action. When we grow, we strengthen, develop, mature and expand. In its creative sense, we bring into being and generate GOD'S perfect will of increase and fruitful lives for HIS loved ones.

Through the HOLY SPIRIT we can activate this simple formula of Pray + Press + Praise = the way out of the **"DRY PLACES"**. *"Take care to live in me, and let me live in you. For a branch cannot produce fruit when severed from the vine. Nor can you be fruitful apart from ME. "Yes, I am the Vine; you are the branches. Whoever lives in ME and I in him shall produce a large crop of fruit. For apart from ME you cannot do a thing. "You didn't choose ME! I chose you! I appointed you to go and produce lovely fruit always, so that no matter what you ask for from the FATHER, using my name, HE will give it to you."* John 15: 4, 5 & 16 The Living Bible

PRAY! This formula starts with our acceptance of GOD as LORD in our lives and acknowledging that we are totally dependent on HIM. We pray without ceasing in every situation we encounter. Many see prayer as weak, spineless and the last resort of out-of-touch people in over their heads. I beg to differ. Prayer is the very first tactic of powerful, resourceful people living in the favor of GOD. Prayer allows mere humans to transcend the supernatural and contend with the forces of evil. Prayer warriors know the secrets of calling upon scriptural promises to bring about triumphant change.

The greatest weapon believers own is the ability to employ faith-laced, fervent and continuous prayer. When we do our part of praying scripture promises to combat troubles, things can turn around holding disaster at bay. Scripture promises are not to remind GOD about HIS word, rather they are to propel us into action. We have the authority to bind or forbid things on earth and those things are forbidden in Heaven. GOD authorizes us to loose or set free things on earth with the assurance that they will be released in Heaven. *"Truly I tell you, whatever you forbid and declare to be improper and unlawful on earth must be what is already forbidden in heaven, and whatever you permit and declare proper and lawful on earth must be what is already permitted in heaven"* Matthew 18:18 Amplified

Our prayer affirms our confidence that everything that GOD allows in our life will work together for our good. We then respond by loving HIM with all of our heart, mind and soul acknowledging that if HE never does anything else for us, we are already blessed to be in the kingdom. HIS HOLY SPIRIT frames our prayers to coincide with GOD'S purpose for our life. *"In the same way, the Spirit helps us in our weakness. We do not know what we ought to pray for, but the Spirit himself intercedes for us with groans that words cannot express."* Romans 8:26 NIV. Most of the time we do not know how we manage to end up in the **"DRY PLACES"** or how long we will stay. We will need GOD'S supernatural help to move on. **We need the Comfort of the HOLY SPIRIT.**

PRESS! We also have to press our way determinedly through, refusing to set up camp in the **"DRY PLACES."** The verb form of the word press means to exert steady weight or force for the purpose of movement. In pressing, we encourage our selves with the promises of GOD and refuse to stagger in doubt, fear and negativity. We must always strive to reach for a higher place in GOD. Troubling times are not battles that any of us need to fight on our own. GOD gave us the gift of the HOLY SPIRIT. HE is our advocate and defender. We must never allow anything to keep us from seeking GOD. Whenever we feel faint and want to give up, that is the time to press and put forth extreme effort to keep going. In our weakness, GOD'S strength is made perfect.

Do not doubt and second-guess the decisions that have bought you to the "**DRY PLACES.**" GOD sees you so continue to press and push yourself forward. Looking back and pinning away for days long gone are counter-productive tactics devised by the enemy to frustrate your progress. Move continually towards GOD, not away from HIM. We must each decide to lay aside every weight the "**DRY PLACES**" puts in our way and press on. Never stop and never quit. As we relentlessly push forward, we are able to maintain our footing in spite of difficulty, obstacles and discouragement.

Like JESUS, we must be about the FATHER'S business. Get out of the "**DRY PLACES**" and do what GOD has called you to do! Grow in your commitment of excellence in everything you do. Serve GOD by leading and lead by serving. Do not shrink back from what GOD has planned for you. Continue to be steadfast and squash any notions of remaining in the "**DRY PLACES.**" There is still so much to accomplish! *"If we are living now by the HOLY SPIRIT'S power, let us follow the HOLY SPIRIT'S leading in every part of our lives"* Galatians 5:25 TLB. **We need the Power of the HOLY SPIRIT.**

PRAISE! Finally, GOD wants us to continue our praise at all times. Our grasp of any situation is limited to our vantage point, but our acknowledgement of GOD'S sovereignty should not be. We can prolong our stay in the "**DRY PLACES**" with a wrong attitude. Failure to always love and trust GOD will hinder our praise. Praise is learning to speak the goodness of the LORD no matter what happens. When we understand the importance of praising the LORD, there will be nothing that we cannot accomplish through HIM. Praise is also a verb and is something we must do. The Bible urges everything that has breath to praise the LORD. It is expressing warm approval, admiration or congratulation. It means to commend, to applaud and to magnify.

When we praise the LORD, we are obediently doing what we were created to do. The Psalmist in the Bible says, "We were created to make HIS praise glorious!" GOD inhabits or dwells in the midst of our sincere praise. HE delights in our praise and rejoices over us. Our praise ushers us into HIS presence and transports us into the realm of the supernatural. Praising GOD lifts our heart and mind far above our troubles. Praise changes us and helps us to remember all of the wonderful things HE has done. Our focus is redirected from ourselves to who GOD is and what HE is able to accomplish in the earth.

Although praising GOD expresses love and releases great joy and peace, praise is also a powerful weapon in spiritual warfare. The secret about spiritual warfare is that the battle is not ours but belongs to the LORD. The truth is when we praise GOD, HIS presence shows up in a mighty way. This sends the enemy running with his imps cowardly scampering behind him. GOD is omnipotent! HE is all-powerful. HE is the Supreme Being that is greater than any force anywhere.

At GOD'S manifested presence, the enemy's schemes turn back, stumble and perish. In the midst of any struggle, our part is passionate praise. The psalmist declared, "I will Bless the LORD at all times, HIS praise shall continually be in my mouth!" (Psalm 34:1 KJV) No matter how things may look, or how bad things may seem, do not fear. Persist in trusting GOD and continually tell how magnificently GOD does what HE does!

Recognize and appreciate the very attributes of GOD and then acknowledge HIS graciousness towards us. When we develop an attitude of gratitude, a mighty breakthrough occurs! "*Though the cherry trees don't blossom and the strawberries don't ripen, Though the apples are worm-eaten and the wheat fields stunted, Though the sheep pens are sheep less and the cattle barns empty, I'm singing joyful praise to GOD. I'm turning cartwheels of joy to my Savior GOD*" Habakkuk 3:17-18 Message. **We need the Unspeakable Joy of the HOLY SPIRIT.**

Throughout this book, we will stop from time to time for a ***PRAISE BREAK!*** GOD deserves glory, honor and the highest praise. Hallelujah! Our praise break allows us to affirm that there is absolutely nothing more important to us than GOD is! You can praise GOD by singing songs celebrating HIS glory. When you praise, you can lift your hands in adoration and total surrender to HIS perfect will for your life. You can clap your hands in praise applauding GOD'S goodness and mercy. You can raise a shout of triumph, acclaiming the victory GOD has wrought over all types of evil. You can even dance before the LORD exuberantly extolling HIS eternal dominion over all that exists. Hallelujah! All who love GOD sing a brand-new song and shout the high praises. Hallelujah!

Whenever you find yourself on the way to the **"DRY PLACES"** my prayer is that you will rely on the HOLY SPIRIT to help you express your love, appreciation, adoration, and reverence to our GOD. Ask GOD to draw you even closer to HIM. Make a commitment for greater intimacy in your relationship with GOD. Tommy Tenney wrote in his book, *Finding Favor with the King* that with relationship one gains access and with intimacy influence! Influence the way you want your life to be by your intimate relationship with GOD.

Expect your intimate relationship with GOD to grant you powerful influence in the world around you. Expect GOD to show HIMSELF strong and mighty in your life. Expect GOD to transport you to brand new places in HIM. Expect your life to be flooded with love, joy, peace and all of the other fruits of the SPIRIT. Expect to continue growing in knowledge. This growth process will strengthen and enlighten you. You will become a person on the rise and on the increase in your overall pleasure and enjoyment of life. Pray, Press and Praise as you *GROW* through the **"DRY PLACES."**

May GOD bless you indeed, as you take this journey away from the **"DRY PLACES."** We may not always have a choice about visiting the **"DRY PLACES"**, but we never, ever have to stay there! *"I know your works. See, I have set before you an open door, and no one can shut it; for you have a little strength, have kept MY word, and have not denied MY name. Revelations 3:8* NKJV

Dear Heavenly Father,

*I pray now for every person who reads this book.
YOU have proclaimed that this word pave the way for
greater depths and increased wisdom for each reader.
May his or her life never be the same from this day forward.
YOUR Word tells us that whatsoever we bind or forbid on
earth is bound in heaven and whatsoever we loose or
set free on earth is loosed in heaven. In the name of JESUS,
forbid any spirit of darkness that would hold the reader
captive in "DRY PLACES" and set free love, joy and peace.
Please send YOUR anointing and grant understanding
in the power of the HOLY SPIRIT.
In JESUS name I pray,*

Amen.

STOP

TAKE A

PRAISE

BREAK!

When you consider the times, GOD'S love and mercy helped, begin to thank and praise HIM!

- ✓ *PRAISE GOD FOR HIS GOODNESS!*

- ✓ *PRAISE GOD BECAUSE HE IS ABLE TO DO EXCEEDINGLY ABUNDANTLY MORE THAN YOU CAN ASK OR THINK!*

- ✓ *PRAISE GOD BECAUSE HE IS SOVEREIGN AND KNOWS WHAT IS BEST FOR YOU!*

PRAYING TIME

When you suddenly discover that you have been transported to the "DRY PLACES" against your will, it is time to pray!

Is anyone among you suffering? He should keep on praying about it. And those who have reason to be thankful should continually be singing praises to the LORD. Is anyone sick? He should call for the elders of the church and they should pray over him and pour a little oil upon him, calling on the LORD to heal him. And their prayer, if offered in faith, will heal him, for the LORD will make him well; and if his sickness was caused by some sin, the LORD will forgive him. James 5: 13-15 TLB

When circumstances produce discouragement, depression and bury us in defeat, prayer transforms our vulnerability into victory. Material things that were lost are replaced and there is help from GOD to begin again. Take comfort in scripture and know that you will make it. Pray always and receive GOD'S help.

CHAPTER ONE

The Desert

Never, never, never give up.
—Winston Churchill

Unless you try to do something beyond
what you have already mastered,
you will never grow.
—Ronald E. Osborn

Life without a purpose is a languid,
drifting thing; every day we ought to
review our purpose, saying to ourselves,
'This day let me make a sound beginning
—Thomas Kempis

When I think of the desert, I can see a land of extreme heat, extreme dryness sudden, flash floods and cold nights. The environment is so harsh that deserts often have names like "Death Valley," "the empty quarter," and "the place from where there is no return." Deserts are usually very, very dry. Even the wettest deserts get less than ten inches of precipitation a year. During the day, many deserts are very hot with temperatures in excess of 100 degrees. Yet at night, the same deserts can have temperatures that are extremely cold.

Some of the famous deserts are the Kalahari Desert in Southern Africa, the Gobi Desert in Mongolia and China, and even the Mojave Desert here in the United States. Among the desert animals are insects, poisonous spiders and reptiles. Most of these animals are nocturnal, sleeping in the heat of the day and coming out at night to eat and hunt.

Even though the most common picture of the desert is miles of sand under the blazing hot sun with very little water, I imagine that at night it is more horrible, gloomy and frightening. Just think of a place with no warmth and deadly animals all about scavenging for food. Imagine the sounds and the smells present.

What I have read about the Sahara desert depicts the extreme case of danger. The Sahara is the world's largest desert at 3.5 million square miles. It covers large parts of North Africa with mountains and rocky areas, gravel plains, salt flats and huge sand dunes. There are several rivers running through the Sahara, of which the Nile and Niger are the most important permanent ones. Most other rivers are seasonal, or filled with water only for short periods often with years in between.

In the Sahara, there is very little rain. Rainfall is usually torrential when it occurs after long dry periods that sometimes last for years. The area used to be lush with green forests and lakes. However, a massive climate change in the early pre-historic times caused the whole place to dry up. Wind and erosion turned the petrified land into sand.

The climate there is one of the harshest in the world. The desiccating and dust-laden winds are sometimes felt north and south of the desert.

Daytime temperatures are high. Heat loss is rapid at night and freezing temperatures are not uncommon.

Overall, being stuck in the Sahara at night has to be a frightening experience with little hope of survival. How long would it take the average person to travel 3.5 million miles on foot? Without shelter or a water supply, is it even possible to travel non-stop? Would the individual be at risk of being devoured by desert creatures? If not eaten, wouldn't they go crazy or die of loneliness? ***Help, LORD JESUS!***

The idea of traveling the desert alone by foot seems hopeless. The chances of survival are very slim and the person attempting such a feat would probably be brought to his or her knees, crawling to continue the journey out. In the event of death, no doubt, the corpse of the misfortunate desert crawler would be picked clean by scavengers.

Such a scene was witnessed by Ezekiel. Ezekiel was a priest as well as a prophet. His account of the vision he experienced while a captive in Babylonia starts in the 37th chapter of Ezekiel. He recounts that the hand of the LORD was upon him as he was brought by the SPIRIT of the LORD to the middle of a valley. The valley was barren and full of many dry bones. The bones appeared to be those of a vast army that fell in battle. Not only was this army defeated, they paid the ultimate price of losing life. They did not receive a decent burial!

Many theologians have taught about the significance of the valley of dry bones. Some say it signifies the punishment of the LORD when an army fights outside HIS will. Others argue that it is really an allegory of how dry and lifeless man is without GOD. A third group explains that this account points up the need for the resurrection power of the HOLY SPIRIT.

The next part of the vision involves a dialogue between GOD and Ezekiel. GOD asks of Ezekiel, "Son of man, can these bones live?" I said, "O Sovereign LORD, you alone know." (Verse 3)

Why do you suppose GOD asked this question of Ezekiel? We know that GOD is omniscient. HE knows everything that is to be known! Certainly, GOD did not need Ezekiel's answer to understand what was going on.

Perhaps, Ezekiel needed the information buried within his answer. GOD told Ezekiel to prophesy to the bones saying, 'Dry bones, hear the word of the LORD!' Ezekiel told the bones that GOD would make breath enter them and that they would come to life.

Ezekiel even proclaimed to the bones that GOD would attach tendons and make flesh appear to cover them with skin. GOD promised to breathe into the bones that they might come to life! Using your imagination, just picture Ezekiel talking over a vast army of dry bones. Imagine these bones bleached by the sun and lying in disarray. Perhaps the bones were so scattered, with an arm here and a leg there, a complete human form could not be found in one place. For the bones to be in such an extreme dry state, one would think that they had been in this condition a very long time.

The final part of the prophesy to the bones was, "Then you will know that I am the LORD." At some level, these bones still had the cognitive ability to reason. (With GOD, all things are possible!)

Ezekiel obeyed GOD and as he prophesied, Ezekiel heard a rattling sound of the bones coming together. Ezekiel saw tendons and flesh as they appeared on the bones. Amazing! Skin also covered the bones, but there was not any breath in them.

I found this part of the vision particularly interesting. Ezekiel was instructed by GOD to prophesy again to the bones. In other words, speak it again. Say to it, "This is what the Sovereign LORD says: Come from the four winds, O breath, and breathe into these slain, that they may live." (Verse 9)

When Ezekiel obeyed, breath entered them; they came to life and stood up on their feet. Once again, they were a vast army. GOD gives the significance of the bones by proclaiming that the bones represented Israel. Instead of a mighty army, the people had become dried up with no hope. They had become bereft and believed that they had been cut off from GOD.

Our Heavenly FATHER knows all about us. Just as HE knew the heart of the people after they had been exiled to Babylon, HE understands when life holds us captive in the **"DRY PLACES."**

GOD told Ezekiel to prophesy to the people. Let them know that they are HIS people. GOD will open up what seemed dead and in the grave. GOD would restore them to the land of Israel. GOD promised to put HIS SPIRIT in them and they would return home to their own land. All of this was done so they would know that the LORD would do just what HE promised.

It is comforting to know that GOD cares so much for you and me that HE will dispatch a message to us when we have been exiled to the "**DRY PLACES.**" GOD knows when we feel hopeless, helpless and ready to give up. GOD always speaks to us at those times to reassure us. HE lets us know that with HIS SPIRIT we can live again. GOD has given each of us the ability to speak to dry, barren and lifeless situations in our lives and call things that are not as if they were.

In the Old Testament times, the HOLY SPIRIT came upon prophet, priests, and kings for a period to equip them for a specific purpose. Today you and I have the promise of the baptism of the HOLY SPIRIT. To be baptized in the HOLY SPIRIT means to be immersed, submerged, and saturated in the HOLY SPIRIT. We never have to be alone because the Spirit of the almighty GOD will live within us!

The indwelling of the HOLY SPIRIT is given to all who have been redeemed or placed in the body of CHRIST. The simple act of believing that JESUS gave HIS life for our sins, repenting then accepting HIM as SAVIOR, grants us the most wonderful gift. The HOLY SPIRIT is our Helper, Comforter, Teacher, and source of Power.

The "**DRY PLACES**" will dehydrate the SPIRIT if you allow it. If you stir up or unleash the gift of the HOLY SPIRIT within you, it will start a regeneration process in you. You can be confident that you are blessed and highly favored of GOD. You have been appointed and anointed to the high places of GOD eternally. The visit to the "**DRY PLACES**" is only temporary. If you do not give up and dry out you will get away from these horrible places and times in your life.

None of us has to remain piled up on a desert wasteland picked cleaned by scavengers. GOD will help us. All we have to do is speak. Use faith when we speak to call forth the promises of GOD. Just as GOD asked Ezekiel, shall your dry bones live again? Will you obey and allow the HOLY SPIRIT to breathe life into you? Will you spring forth with new vigor and a greater sense of gusto for all life yet has to offer?

Love, Live and Enjoy Life by Dr. Creflo A. Dollar teaches that love is a decision. It is a force like dynamite. Love is the powerful and explosive force behind faith. Grow, produce, emerge and surface again knowing GOD loves you completely, lavishly and eternally. Love GOD in turn with all your heart, mind and soul. Remember your visits to the "**DRY PLACES**" are only temporary!

Dear Heavenly Father,

Thank YOU for loving me enough to dispatch YOUR HOLY SPIRIT to breathe life into me. I cast upon YOU every care in my life for I know YOU care for me. Whenever I feel dry and barren again, I will remember that all conditions are only temporary but YOUR love for me is everlasting. The gift of YOUR HOLY SPIRIT is my source of power and comfort. In the mighty name of JESUS, I pray,

Amen.

CHAPTER TWO

The Lie

I have a higher and greater standard of principle. Washington could not lie. I can lie but I won't.
—Mark Twain (1835-1910)

Sin has many tools, but a lie is the handle which fits them all.
—Anonymous

A lie can travel half way around the world while the truth is putting on its shoes.
—Mark Twain

There is nothing like a day at the beach to lift my sagging spirits and gloomy days. Sitting out at the earth's edges it seems, a sense of well being overtakes me as I observe the vastness of the skies overhead. I look out as far as the eye can see where the ocean meets sky and beyond the roaring waves. The distinct sound of sea gulls flying around, waves crashing in and the laughter of people all around is what I hear.

There is a salty ocean smell and even though the bright sun is overhead, the air feels moist and fresh. People are milling about in bright colored swim gear. Little children are building sand castles and lovers are walking the water's edge holding hands. Reclining in a beach lounge chair under the shade of a huge umbrella heightens the enjoyment. I love the Caribbean beaches where the faint sounds of steel drums can be heard.

Just think. The water is so cool, refreshing and inviting with sparkling hues of blue and sea green that it beckons you to get up and get in. Can't you imagine stripping off your cover up gear and running out to ride the waves? You make a mad dash leaping to make a great splash and land belly first into a sand dune! "What happened?" you sputter through a mouth full of sand. Not only have you sustained physical injury from your disastrous fall, but also you are humiliated. It was not real. It was only a mirage. How could you have been so fooled?

Maybe you needed the day at the beach to fill a deep longing created by the "**DRY PLACES**". On the other hand, perhaps you have been in the "**DRY PLACES**" so long that you would have done anything to get out. Maybe you had begun to be suspicious of this day at the beach outing but were so desperate for a change, that you ignored your better judgment. You were deceived. It was all a lie and none of it was real.

That is a common mistake made by many. Think about the Bible story of Samson and Delilah in sixteenth chapter of Judges starting at the fourth verse. If we read the background information about Samson in the proceeding chapters, we learn that he was born to a barren woman who had been visited by an angel of GOD.

We learn that Samson was chosen by GOD from birth and was raised with specific godly instructions that gave him great strength. After all, of the many miraculous things GOD had done in his life he fell in love with an evil woman of questionable moral character named Delilah.

The rulers of the Philistines convinced her to betray Samson for eleven hundred pieces of silver. (Verse 5, CEV) They suggested that she trick Samson into revealing the source of his strength. The Philistines wanted to capture and kill Samson in retaliation for the damage done to their nation.

Delilah agreed to this scheme and decided to use her beauty to beguile Samson into revealing his secret. Delilah asked Samson to tell her the source of his great strength and how he could be tied up and subdued. Samson toyed with her and said if anyone tied him with seven new bowstrings that had not been dried; he would be as weak as any other man would.

The Philistines gave her the seven new bowstrings looking forward to capturing Samson. Delilah was so convinced that she had it like that with Samson that she even arranged for Philistine soldiers to hide into the very room where she was "*entertaining*" Samson. She tied up Samson **(Of course he allowed her to)** and yelled out that the Philistines were attacking. Samson snapped the bow strings as easily as a piece of string snaps when it comes close to a flame. Samson's secret of his strength went undiscovered.

Delilah berated Samson and said, "You lied and made me look like a fool. Now tell me, how can I really tie you up? **(We probably would ask at this point, why she wanted to know.)** Samson however made up another answer and told Delilah if anyone tied him up with new ropes that have never been used; he would become as weak as any other man would.

For the second time Delilah tried to orchestrate Samson's capture. She took new ropes and tied Samson's arms with them. With men again hidden in the room, she shouted that the Philistines were attacking. What a Fake! What a Traitor! What a Phony! Samson snapped the ropes off his arms as if they were threads. By then Delilah was exasperated. "You're still lying and making a fool of me. Tell me how I can tie you up!"(Verse 13, CEV) Notice that although she was the one deceiving Samson, she still thought he owed her the truth!

Samson made up another elaborate fable and told her if she wove his seven braids into the threads on a loom and nailed the loom to a wall, he would become as weak as any other man would. This time Delilah waited until Samson was sleeping to take the seven braids of his head and weave as he instructed. *(Ha-Ha fooled again!)* That time when she shouted that the Philistines were attacking, Samson woke up and pulled the loom free.

After three times, most of us would have gotten a clue that this person really does not love us. When someone really cares about us, he or she does not require us to jump through hoops to prove our love. Rather, that person wants only what is best for us and would not dream of doing anything that would hurt us.

Delilah manipulated, cajoled and cried to Samson. She said, "You claim to love me, but you don't mean it! You've made me look like a fool three times now, and you still haven't told me why you are so strong." (Verse 15, CEV) That same verse in the Bible depicts Delilah as a nagging shrew that pestered Samson day after day wearing him down until he could not stand any more of it.

Finally, Samson told her everything. He told her that he had been set apart to GOD from birth and never had his haircut. Samson told her that if his head were shaved, his strength would leave him and he would become as weak as any other man would.

We are not surprised that Delilah sent word to the rulers of the Philistines to come back to her home once more. She was so satisfied that she had conquered him that the soldiers came back with her silver payoff. Delilah kicked up her seduction ploys a notch and had Samson sleeping on her lap like a little baby. She signaled to one of the Philistine men when she began cutting off his seven braids.

By the time, she finished shaving his head, and Samson's strength was gone. This time when she called out that the Philistines were attacking, he awoke from his sleep and thought he would go about as before and shake himself free. Samson did not know that the LORD had left him.

The Philistines captured him, gouged out his eyes and took him down to Gaza. They bound Samson with bronze shackles but did not kill him right away. Samson was locked up in prison and was forced into slave labor grinding grain. Over a period while enduring vile treatment, the hair on Samson's head began to grow again.

The Philistines assembled at their temple to celebrate Samson's defeat and to offer sacrifices to their false god. The temple was crowded. All of the rulers of the Philistines were there, and on the roof were about three thousand men and women. They made up a chant crediting their god for delivering Samson into their hands. They went so far as to bring him out before a large crowd to make fun of him.

Samson had the final tee-hee-hee though. While they were in high spirits, ridiculing him, Samson *prayed* asking GOD to remember him. He asked the LORD to make him strong one last time so that he could take revenge. Samson had asked the young man who lead him around by the hand to place him near the central columns of the temple so that he could rest.

GOD heard his prayer and strengthened Samson again. As Samson stood between the two middle supporting columns and shouted, "Let me die with the Philistine." (Verse 30,) Then Samson pushed with all his might, and down came the temple on the rulers and all the people in it.

Like Samson, whenever people allow false relationships to govern their lives, they will find themselves trapped in the "**DRY PLACES**.' These false relationships have been given the power by the individual to inflict pain and dole out joy. False relationships will cause a person to determine the worth of his or her life totally on the basis or the whims of someone else.

False relationships are deceptive and have unwittingly been given the power to destroy lives. Often times, individuals who seek fulfillment from false relationships will do anything to cling to a good standing in the false relationship. Little do they know that their acceptance in the relationship is really in their own mind. Numerous times clues will be given that the relationship is false, but often people are reluctant to see it.

False relationships constantly give mixed signals. They are pleasant and inviting at times. Then with no warning, they are cool and distant. False relationships have levels of affections that can only be obtained by arbitrary maneuverings. In other words, like in the case of Delilah, affection is withheld and only sparingly dispersed as a reward. This type of seesaw behavior keeps the poor unfortunate person on edge constantly trying to satisfy the sadistic whims of the false relationship's manipulator.

Do you remember when JESUS entered Jerusalem riding on a donkey? The people were so exuberant that they laid their coats on the ground and spread palm leaves before HIM. They cried, "Hosanna!" and gave HIM high praise. If you were to look only on appearances, you would conclude that this crowd really loved JESUS! Yet, a few days later, some of the same people were a part of a vicious mob demanding that JESUS be crucified. **(They loved HIM one moment and kicked HIM to the curb the next!)**

False relationships breed inferiority/superiority complexes. Rather than focusing on serving GOD, the person with the inferiority complex never feels good enough. That person's entire focus is on himself or herself wondering what they can do for the few moments when they receive a smile from the partner in the false relationship. Even if it inflicts pain, there is nothing too unscrupulous or distasteful for the victim to do or say to earn brownie points. **(Have mercy GOD.)**

"Be especially careful when you are trying to be good so that you don't make a performance out of it. It might be good theater, but the GOD who made you won't be applauding." Matthew 6:1 Message

On the other hand, the person with the superiority complex is unhappy too. He or she can never receive the blessings of GOD while assuming this role of falsely bestowing favor on the life of another. This type of person is extremely fickle and has a difficult time sustaining relationships with others. Relationships to them are only worthwhile if there is something they can gain. Rarely are they interested in generously sowing into the life of another. Rather, the very least that they can possibly do for another is the path that they always choose.

GOD sees the motives of both parties in false relationship. GOD is a jealous GOD and will not share HIS glory with another. If the *"Superior"* person uses manipulation, insincerity and intimidation to control the life of another, GOD will execute judgment. If the *"Inferior"* person uses bribery, flattery and eye-service to please another, GOD will also execute judgment.

GOD wants us to be in true fellowship with one another. JESUS tells us in John 13:34-35 NIV *"A new command I give you: Love one another. As I have loved you, so you must love one another. By this all men will know that you are my disciples, if you love one another."*

The quickest way out of the "**DRY PLACES**" is to enter into a real relationship with GOD empowered by the HOLY SPIRIT. It is genuine! GOD has loved us with an everlasting love and wants what is best for us. It is HIS desire to bless us and to fill our lives with good things. GOD desires that we have healthy relationships with others and enjoy our lives to the fullest.

Author Joyce L. Rodgers in her book, *FATAL Distractions,* declares that distractions are lies from the pit of hell. They are sent by the enemy to pull us away from our destiny. GOD grants us the spirit of discernment so that we do not have to be fooled by people who want to harm us. A right relationship with GOD will help us to develop right relationships with others. By HIS SPIRIT, we will be able to pray for, honor, encourage, accept, live in peace with, comfort, forgive, serve, and be kind to one another. *Beloved, I pray that you may prosper in all things and be in health, just as your soul prospers. 3 John 2* NKJV

Learn to grow in genuine, unconditional love for others. Learn to love GOD first, and then loving yourself and others will not be difficult. Developing a healthy relationship with GOD through the HOLY SPIRIT will shorten your times in the "**DRY PLACES**." They really are not nice places to visit so you certainly do not have to stay there!

Dear Heavenly FATHER,

*I pray for YOUR discernment.
Help me to make good choices as I enter into
a deeper relationship with YOU.
Please, examine my heart and help me to
operate with pure motives. I now forbid deception
at any level and false relationships
from this day forward. I commit to be in true
fellowship with others within YOUR kingdom.
In the precious name of JESUS I pray,*

Amen.

STOP

TAKE A

PRAISE

BREAK!

When you consider the times, GOD freed you from deceitful people, begin to thank and praise HIM!

- ✓ *PRAISE GOD FOR GIVING YOU WISDOM!*

- ✓ *PRAISE GOD FOR TRUE FRIENDS!*

- ✓ *PRAISE GOD FOR DELIVERING YOU FROM THE SNARE OF THE ENEMY!*

CHAPTER THREE

The Pain

*One word frees us of all the weight and
pain of life: that word is love.*
—Sophocles

*Forgiveness does not change the past, but it
does enlarge the future.*
—Paul Boese

The pain passes, but the beauty remains.
—Pierre Auguste Renoir

Most of the time when we have been hurt by another, we are totally unprepared for the undeserved blow. It could have been actions taken or not taken that caused the offense. Maybe it was words spoken or things left unsaid that brought on feelings of abandonment and rejection. Maybe a close loved one entered into a relationship with someone else that made you feel cheated and betrayed. Maybe you have been totally ignored and your worth discounted.

You feel so victimized that the hurt goes deep enough to inflict constant, acute and throbbing pain. It may be so painful that you examine your body from time to time to see if you are actually bleeding from your wounds. You may be tempted to question GOD. How will YOU receive the glory in this situation LORD? How can this work together for my good? It seems so unfair!!!!

Nights are spent tossing and turning as your mind continually replays all of the horrible things that have transpired. The more you think about them, the more words like, "Dread!" "Disaster!" "Doom!" rage from within. These emotions banish us to the **"DRY PLACES"** in a morass of self-pity and raw remorse. Self-recriminations may begin to torment you. "How could I have been so foolish, so trusting and so oblivious to what was occurring in my life? Why couldn't I correctly decipher the handwriting on the wall?" you may ask yourself.

Once again, you have been hijacked to the **"DRY PLACES"** and you do not want to be there. How can someone hurt me this way and merrily go about his or her daily life? Do they have a conscience or is this all my fault for caring too much? I expected better treatment than this. You may make deals with yourself by deciding, if I ever get over this, I will never let these people hurt me again!

The only way we can hope to leave the **"DRY PLACES"** is to realize that people who are already hurting themselves hurt other people. If you were to know the secrets behind the façade, you would realize that everybody has something that they are dealing with themselves. The **"DRY PLACES"** make you think that you are the only one hurting and that everyone else has it all together. Not so, when JESUS was being crucified, HE took the time to pray for HIS tormenter. HE asked the FATHER to forgive them because they did not know what they were doing.

The temptation to retreat and withdraw from everyone is your prevailing thought. Since you feel rejected, you might as well reject everyone else around you, often hurting those who love you most! If you decide to grin and bear the pain, it could eat you up inside. Making the decision to deal with the pain may cause temporary discomfort; however, it will start the process for leaving the "**DRY PLACES**"

Consider JESUS' teaching about how we are to handle our relationship with other people. The Sermon on the Mount also gives instructions for resolving conflict. The Message translation and the New International Version of the Bible are contrasted to help make these instructions plain so that we can apply them to situations we face each day.

"You're blessed when you're at the end of your rope. With less of you, there is more of GOD and his rule. Message

"Blessed are the poor in spirit, for theirs is the kingdom of heaven." NIV (Mathew 5:3)

Many times in the work of the LORD, you will face periods of time that will challenge your fortitude. Stick with it and do not quit. Human flesh can cause you to say, "I'm out of here! I don't have to stay where I am not wanted!" Do not give in to this type of reasoning. Remain steadfast reminding yourself that you serve to please GOD not man. Anytime GOD calls you to work for HIM, HE supplies what you need through HIS HOLY SPIRIT to get it done. The HOLY SPIRIT is your Helper and GOD will reward your service. Your life is precious to GOD and it is HIS desire for you to prosper and be in health as your soul prospers.

"You're blessed when you feel you've lost what is most dear to you. Only then can you be embraced by the One most dear to you. Message,

"Blessed are those who mourn, for they will be comforted". NIV (Mathew 5:4)

Loss is a major vehicle used to transport people to the "**DRY PLACES.**" After loosing a job or position, many are so bereft that they in turn loose their identities. The way that they have seen themselves is in direct correlation with what they have obtained. Throughout my ministry, I have counseled many who had faced career set backs or complete loss of income. They were afraid that they would not be able to make ends meet. Little did they know that GOD is our source, not man. Jobs can bring about temporary income but only GOD can grant eternal favor.

When the loss is created by death or divorce, do not forget that GOD will dispatch the Comforter to soothe your broken heart. In *Five Cries of Grief* by Merton P and A. Irene Strommen, they share their testimony of the loss of a son. According to their experience, death's pain is as if something had been physically wrenched, ripped and torn out of their bodies. The pain was so intense. It left them unable to understand how something so awful could happen to them. Yet in the midst of the grief, they continued to trust GOD.

Like the Strommen's, many questions may run through your mind during your period of mourning, but remember your loving Heavenly FATHER wants you to grow through every heart-rending experience. Be assured that you will get through it. Everyday will get better. You are not alone because GOD is always with you. In time the pain will subside.

Through HIS HOLY SPIRIT, GOD will turn the times of weeping into times of joy. If you simply give your loss to GOD in prayer, your joy in the LORD will bubble over and escape in audible expressions. Think about all of your beautiful memories with a lost loved one. Remember funny things said and done. Do not forget some of the favorite things you did together. Let go, thanking GOD that you had the privilege of knowing your loved one. With GOD'S embrace, you can smile again!

In the case of divorce, refuse to become bitter. Do not concentrate on the bad times. Rather, focus on the pleasant things that happened within the marriage. Try to find at least three good things that came out of the relationship and give GOD glory for that!

"You're blessed when you're content with just who you are—no more, no less. That's the moment you find yourself proud owners of everything that can't be bought. Message

Blessed are the meek, for they will inherit the earth. NIV (Mathew 5:5)

Look at how the Message Bible uses the word *content* to help us understand the term meek in this text. Words like happy, satisfied, pleased, fulfilled, glad, joyful, blissful, delighted, rewarded, and fortunate help paint the picture of the posture in which we should remain. Whenever life delivers a blow, contentment will help us move from dryness in the "**DRY PLACES**" to looking ahead with hope that the pain will subside in time.

Many times, it appears that if you are meek, people around you can mistake your stance as weak. Although these two words rhyme, they are spelled differently. There are two e's in meek, which stand for Eternal Enjoyment! In other words, no matter how your life may appear to the uninformed outsider, you are deeply loved by the FATHER and have been promoted to a place of favor with HIM.

"You're blessed when you've worked up a good appetite for GOD. He's food and drink in the best meal you'll ever eat. Message

Blessed are those who hunger and thirst for righteousness, for they will be filled. NIV (Mathew 5:6)

Sometime even the best intentions blow up in our faces. Have you ever unwittingly hurt someone with the words you have spoken or with something, you have done? Never in a million years would you cause them pain, yet the very thing you did or said **(seemingly for their own good)** backfired.

I can remember jokingly making a comment to a colleague who became highly incensed. I was kidding about the extra pounds I had put on by overeating. While berating myself, he became highly offended. **(He is overweight too)** Little did I know that my comments were viewed as a put down on him. Oh why, oh why, did I open my big mouth? It was difficult to speak around my own foot in my mouth, but speak I did. My apology had to make him realize that I was merely speaking about myself. No matter what I said though, the awkward situation could not be fixed. The more I spoke the deeper the hole I dug for my self. Help me LORD JESUS!

Sometimes we do not know what we should say. That is why we have the HOLY SPIRIT as our teacher. If our hearts have been fixed by GOD'S SPIRIT and we take everything to HIM in prayer, even this situation can be healed. GOD sees our motivations and can give us the peace to refrain from speaking at times. We do sometimes, talk our way into the "**DRY PLACES**" but we do not have to cleverly talk our way out of it. GOD will give us the wisdom to say the right thing. If we are truly thirsty for GOD, HE will forgive our mistakes and fill us with HIS goodness.

"You're blessed when you care. At the moment of being "careful," you find yourselves cared for. Message

Blessed are the merciful, for they will be shown mercy. NIV (Mathew 5:7)

There are times when you have it in your authority to execute punishment to those who have offended you. You may have the opportunity to get even with someone who caused injury to someone you care about. Little does the offender know that you are fully aware of the entire story about their misdeeds and could make his or her life miserable. Maybe then they would think twice before their ever did that deed again to anyone else.

That is a course of action that could be taken; however, it forfeits our own blessings. Do not forget, we are fortunate recipients of GOD'S mercy. Looking back over your life, you may remember things you have done that deserved punishment. Mercy was extended to you so in turn you should extend it to others. We will reap what we sow. When we sow love, mercy and forgiveness to others, we constantly harvest those results in our life from GOD. Realize that by showing compassion to someone else, we are imitating CHRIST and pleasing GOD.

"You're blessed when you get your inside world—your mind and heart—put right. Then you can see GOD in the outside world." Message.

"Blessed are the pure in heart, for they will see GOD." NIV (Mathew 5:8)

One of the most common mistakes that people in relationship make when trying to resolve a conflict is to assign negative motives to their partners. Most of the time, past hurts or residual pain will cause us to pile up old issues upon new pain.

Even if the new situation has nothing to do with the old ones, past hurts will cause us to feel that our partners in relationship will always look for a way to hurt us. We reason within ourselves that they are never happy unless someone else is down. We must stop the madness and try to always give the other person the benefit of the doubt.

My former pastor and good friend taught a group of ministers that if ever he was late or could not be present at a meeting, one is to always assume that he is somewhere doing good deeds. This rule of thumb is the same way we should govern ourselves in relationship with others. Refuse to see the bad in anyone, only the good. Even if a person actually meant to injure, their actions can be filtered through the FATHER'S love. When this happens, your vantage point becomes so pure that you only see GOD at work in your life. What the enemy meant to curse you, GOD turns around supernaturally to bless you.

"You're blessed when you can show people how to cooperate instead of compete or fight. That is when you discover who you really are, and your place in GOD'S family. Message

Blessed are the peacemakers, for they will be called sons of GOD. NIV (Mathew 5:9)

Have you ever been confident about your ability to do something? Maybe in school you played on a sporting team or academic team. Maybe when it was your turn up at bat, or to pitch, or run, or spell; your teammates went wild with encouraging applause. They cheered, "You can do it!" Even if this has never happened in your life you can imagine, it can't you?

When the best teammates face their opponents, they banish away fear. They are confident in their skills and know that they have spent hours practicing for such a time as this. They know that without confidence they are already defeated. They far out-shine the competition because they know who they are.

So, it is with us once we have been accepted in the Beloved. As children of GOD, we do not have to compete or fight others for our position in CHRIST. Rather, we can encourage and inspire others to excel on GOD'S team. Let GOD put us where HE wants us. We can bloom where we have been planted; even in the **"DRY PLACES"** Ever hear of a desert flower, or the Rose of Sharon? I have read that both are refreshing sights to weary travelers. We are to be just like JESUS, always eager to extend the renewing essence of peace to others.

"You're blessed when your commitment to GOD provokes persecution. The persecution drives you even deeper into GOD'S kingdom. Message

Blessed are those who are persecuted because of righteousness, for theirs is the kingdom of heaven. NIV (Mathew 5:10)

Ever hear the cliché, take a licking and keep on ticking? When you rely on the HOLY SPIRIT, that slogan takes on a completely new meaning. Sometimes persecution can drive you whimpering to the "**DRY PLACES.**" It can be so painful that you may feel that you will surely lose your sanity. Do not forget that the HOLY SPIRIT is also your keeper. In other words, HE can hold you so firmly that you will not lose a grip on your sanity. He can allow the "**DRY PLACES** to be where you "lick" your wounds so that you can keep on ticking!

What the enemy meant for your harm by using unscrupulous and vindictive people against you, GOD *will* use in your favor to catapult you into a place of great blessings! Instead of torment, it will become a place of renewal, revival and rejuvenation. *When a man's ways are pleasing to the LORD, He makes even his enemies live at peace with him.* Proverbs 16:7 NIV

"You're familiar with the old written law, "Love your friend,' and its unwritten companion, "Hate your enemy.' I'm challenging that. I'm telling you to love your enemies. Let them bring out the best in you, not the worst. When someone gives you a hard time, respond with the energies of prayer." Message

"You have heard that it was said, 'Love your neighbor and hate your enemy.' But I tell you: Love your enemies and pray for those who persecute you." NIV (Mathew 5:11)

Have you ever felt the effects of someone in your life that goes out of their way to be unpleasant towards you? If unpleasant people had their way, they would only wish bad things upon GOD'S people and would relish their downfall. The malevolence and ill will cultivated by these enemies would be boundless. If you were to fret about it, you would become very angry and could feel victimized by the treatment you must sometimes endure.

This verse however, reminds the body of believers that our conduct should not be in retaliation to another's negativity. We should each day decide to act as unto the LORD. When our actions are based on love towards other people, GOD is pleased with us. Indeed pray for your enemies and in your prayer ask GOD to help you to forgive them. Forgiveness is the act of forgiving. It is something that one chooses to *do*. It is a willingness to give up the desire to punish or get even. It holds no hard feelings and releases the perceived debt. It cancels the penalty.

Forgiveness brings great peace in hurtful situations, and refuses to take offense or become resentful, annoyed, or repelled by others. Forgiveness will allow us to be loving, merciful, sympathetic, tender, responsive, and compassionate toward those who have offended. Forgiveness will shorten our stay in the "**DRY PLACES.**"

Self-preservation and paranoia may cause you to identify someone in your life as a frienemy. A **FRIENEMY** is someone who is not really your friend but not quite your enemy. This is a person who when given any opportunity and without provocation, will always devise ways to cause you pain. Do not worry though. Ask GOD to help you see this person through Godly love. Try to make every effort to live in peace with everybody. Ask the HOLY SPIRIT to help you.

The "**DRY PLACES**" are homes to bitter, resentful and critical people. Make the choice not to be a part of that group. Refuse to take offense at things said or done to you by others. As you grow, the love of GOD will flourish and expand within you. It will make your attitude so sweet that you will not fit in the "**DRY PLACES!**"

Dear Heavenly FATHER,

*I let go of all bitterness, resentment,
envying, strife, and unkindness in any form.
I forgive everyone who has trespassed against me
so that YOU can forgive me my trespasses.
I ask YOU to forgive and release all
who have wronged and hurt me.
I forgive and release them too.
Deal with them in YOUR mercy
and loving-kindness. I invoke blessings
upon them and pray for their happiness.
I implore YOUR blessings and favor upon them.
From this moment on, I commit to walk in love,
to seek peace, to live in agreement,
and to conduct myself toward others in a
manner that is pleasing to YOU.
In JESUS powerful name,*

Amen.

CHAPTER FOUR

The Fear

"Courage is not the absence of fear, but rather the judgment that something else is more important than fear."
—Ambrose Redmoon

"So, first of all, let me assert my firm belief that the only thing we have to fear is fear itself—nameless, unreasoning, unjustified terror which paralyzes needed efforts to convert retreat into advance."
—Franklin D. Roosevelt

He who is not everyday conquering some fear has not learned the secret of life."
—Ralph Waldo Emerson

The background music used to set up a horror movie is usually brilliant and created to maximize terror. The composers know that the human imagination is a great source for all types of hidden fears. If the orchestras can hit the right string of musical chords, a person's five senses along with his or her fertile imagination will do the job of causing an adrenalin surge of fear. Palms may sweat, hearts will pump faster and with irregular beats, and movie goers may collectively hold their breath dreading what may come next.

In the movie Jaws, each time the great killer shark was about to strike, the scary music would start. Da-Dump, Da-Dump. Da-Dump, Da-Dump, Da-Dump! Faster and faster; louder and louder the ominous tones would resound. As it reached the crescendo, the shark would strike, devouring its victim. Each time this took place the theatre audience would scream in frightful panic.

Often times, I watch movies like this with my hands over my eyes asking my husband, "Now what's happening?" Too afraid to uncover my eyes and see for myself, I did not want to miss all of the action. Fear and curiosity would be in competition for my attention with fear winning out most of the time. My husband and I discovered that if we wanted an enjoyable movie date, perhaps we should skip horror flicks all together.

This strategy worked well for the movies, but in real life, I did not always get the chance to orchestrate the events when something horrible happened in my life. My choices for movies are always romances, comedies, and dramas in that order. I stay away from tearjerkers, scary movies, and action themes with a lot of violence. Life however, can cause tears to flow, terrible things to happen, and violent incidents to occur.

Even when there is not a threat of imminent danger, many people are plagued with internal fears. They can literally quake in their boots with the news that their employer wants to set up a meeting with them. Reactions could remind you of a summons to the principle's office back in grade school. Fearful over active imaginations always suppose the worst as high anxiety kicks in. Dread, a by-product of fear, will rob every one of peace and calm with worse case scenarios and anticipation of what can go wrong in the future. Inwardly fear causes us to shrink from the very thought of a face-to-face meeting with our employer as all types of anxiety plague our mind.

Suppose this meeting brings about a pay reduction or a complete loss of income? Maybe the employer prefers another and will promote someone else. Maybe the employer never liked me in the first place and has some complaints or criticism to use as an excuse to get rid of me. Maybe the employer is threatened by my knowledge and wants to hold me back. Hmmm, maybe the rumors are true, that the employer is really a very unscrupulous person out to get anyone who does not brown nose and is not a yes man. Maybe . . . .

Whoa! Look how unchecked fear can get out of hand. Fear of failure and rejection can be turned up to such a high degree that the employee can work his or her nerves into an agitated state before the meeting. What could have been a pleasant experience becomes fraught with trepidation, tension and paranoia.

Often, fear can cause us to miss the positive things in our lives. Instead of seeing the good, fear causes us to focus on the negative. As Christians, we are not to allow fear to rule our lives. Perfect love for JESUS CHRIST allows us to cast out all fear. We have the authority to confidently face fearful situations armed with the knowledge that the greatest power is on GOD'S side.

Look at the story of Hezekiah who had been king of Judah for over fourteen years when King Sennacherib of Assyria, invaded the country. We start reading this account in the thirty-sixth chapter of Isaiah. We learn that this fierce King captured every fortified city except Jerusalem.

This King was so cocky that he sent his henchmen to three of Hezekiah's highest officers to threaten and ridicule them. The henchmen stood outside the city gate and delivered a threat to Hezekiah and the whole nation. They lied and said that they were doing the LORD'S bidding to come up and destroy the land.

"Don't let Hezekiah fool you-nothing he can do will save you. Don't let him talk you into trusting in the LORD by telling you the LORD won't let you be conquered by the king of Assyria." (Verses 14 & 15 TLB)

The threats were so vile that it preyed on the weaknesses of the people by promising to honor their cowardly surrender. For a period, those who gave the king a token of surrender would be allowed to keep their own vineyards. Besides, the people were also chided with the challenge that they could not muster together 2,000 men to fight for them even with the horses supplied for them! Those messengers of doom bragged about the other nations that they had defeated. In their estimation, no god was able to stand against them.

Though terribly frightened, the people had been instructed that they were not to answer a word and when everything was told to Hezekiah, he tore off his clothes in sorrow. Hezekiah had his leaders to join with him in the outward expression of sorrow by dressing in sackcloth.

Hezekiah sought counsel from Isaiah, GOD'S prophet. Hezekiah wanted Isaiah to know that not only had the nation been threatened, but also the LORD had been insulted. *(When you really love the LORD, it will grieve you when HE has been insulted)* Then Hezekiah asked the man of GOD to pray. He felt that if Isaiah the prophet prayed, that GOD would do something about this grave impending doom.

When the leaders told Isaiah the concerns of Hezekiah, the prophet reassured them with words from GOD. Isaiah told them to tell Hezekiah not to worry about the insulting things that had been said about GOD. GOD promised to upset the king with rumors about what is happening in his own country. GOD'S word from the prophet let Hezekiah know that the king of Assyria would die a violent death in his own country.

In the midst of trying to encourage himself, Hezekiah received a note from the King of Assyria with more threats and taunts. *"Don't let this GOD you trust in fool you by promising that Jerusalem will not be captured by the king of Assyria!"* (Verse 10, TLB) The note even arrogantly listed the other kings with their kingdoms that the Assyrians had defeated and promised to do the same to Hezekiah.

Hezekiah was so distraught when he had the letter read that he went to the house of the LORD, and spread it before the altar. Hezekiah prayed unto the LORD asking for help. Hezekiah started his prayer by acknowledging GOD as creator of everything. This part of the prayer was for Hezekiah's benefit and reiterated the fact that all power was in GOD'S hand. Acknowledgement of GOD'S creative greatness gives reassurance and confidence to the petitioner. Next, Hezekiah asked GOD to incline HIS ear towards him that GOD might hear all that was being said. Hezekiah asked GOD to open HIS eyes to see all that the King of Assyria was doing in reproach of GOD. In prayer, Hezekiah confessed that all of the destruction that Assyria boasted about was true yet he asked GOD to save them and keep HIS people safe. Hezekiah's prayer got results because it started by acknowledging GOD'S power and expressed Hezekiah's trust, appreciation and dependence on GOD. After doing so, Hezekiah confidently made his request in the proper frame of mind.

Often when trouble comes, it can send us to the **"DRY PLACES"** imprisoned by fear. Instead of moving swiftly to our source of deliverance, we can prolong our stay by wallowing in dread and crying about all that has happened to us. Hezekiah immediately enlisted others to join him in prayer. The remarkable example for us is that Hezekiah was also a king yet was not too busy to pray himself. Scripture reminds us that the fervent and effectual prayers of righteous people will greatly help in any situation. GOD has given us the authority through the very powerful name of JESUS to bind, prevent and forbid things on the earth. GOD will honor in heaven the prayers uttered in faith. No matter how bad the situation, we can take a lesson from Hezekiah and pray.

The prophet sent GOD'S answer to Hezekiah promising that the king of Assyria would never enter Jerusalem. GOD promised to protect them for the sake of HIS honor. GOD sent an angel to the camp of the Assyrians and killed one hundred eighty-five thousand in one night. The deflated King of Assyria retreated to the city of Nineveh and lived there until his death. The irony of it is this king was murdered by two of his sons while he was in the temple worshipping his false god. Just as GOD spoke it, that defeated king died a violent death.

If you are not on the LORD'S side, I would advise you to be very afraid. You are not headed to a good end. It may appear that you are getting away with a sinful lifestyle for a little while, but the end will only lead to disaster. It is not too late to turn your life around. You can ask for forgiveness, believe in JESUS CHRIST and get rid of fear.

If you are now on the LORD'S side and incidents in your life have you shaking in fear in the "**DRY PLACES**," pray. Pray that through the fear induced haze; you recognize what a powerful GOD you serve. Pray for GOD'S help out off the "**DRY PLACES**". Let Hezekiah be your example. You cannot face your trouble alone. Remember, GOD has not given us the spirit of fear, but one that produces love, power and a sound mind.

Troubling times are not battles that any of us need to fight on our own. We have been given the gift of the HOLY SPIRIT. HE is our advocate and defender. We must never allow anything to keep us from seeking GOD in prayer. There is nothing too great; nothing too enormous; nothing too colossal or nothing too terrible for prayer. There is also nothing too dreadful or distressing; nothing too awkward or embarrassing; nothing too shocking or appalling and nothing too insignificant to take to our GOD. If it concerns you and me, it concerns GOD.

Anyone who picks a fight with any one of us picks a fight with GOD, the All-Powerful. When the enemy believes that he has knocked us down for the count, we will resurface when we let GOD transport us through HIS spirit out of life's "**DRY PLACES**."

Dear Heavenly FATHER,

*I love YOU and I thank YOU.
I know that YOU are all knowing, all-powerful
and are everywhere. There is nothing happening in my life
that YOU do not know about. I know that YOU care for me
so I give to YOU my fears and the things that have hurt me.
I trust YOU to work it all out for my good. I encourage
myself from this day forward with the many
wonderful promises YOU have given me.
I banish the spirit of fear and embrace the love;
power and the sound mind YOU have granted me.
In the sweet, adorable name of JESUS I pray,*

Amen.

STOP

TAKE A
PRAISE
BREAK!

When you consider the times, GOD rescued you from fear, dread and anxiety, begin to thank and praise HIM!

- ✓ *PRAISE GOD BECAUSE HE HEARD YOUR CRY!*

- ✓ *PRAISE GOD FOR NEVER LEAVING YOU ALONE!*

- ✓ *PRAISE GOD FOR REMOVING THE STING OF PAST HURTS AND DISAPPOINTMENTS!*

PRESS ON

> **When you feel you are stuck in "DRY PLACES" and cannot get out, press! Refuse to become immobile. If you purpose in your heart to press onward, you will find that even your tiny steps have made forward progress. Face each day with the determination to gain new ground. Know that because HE lives you can face your tomorrows. Let these times in "DRY PLACES" squeeze out of you faithfulness, trust and the assurance that GOD knows what HE is doing with YOU. Do not give in to the temptation to question, murmur and complain. Do not become impatient and discouraged. Let GOD keep you in the palm of HIS hand during these times as HIS countenance smiles upon you. Stay sweet and be confident that the effort you put forward will be rewarded with GOD'S richest blessings upon your life!**

Not that I have already obtained all this, or have already been made perfect, but I *press* on to take hold of that for which CHRIST JESUS took hold of me. Brothers, I do not consider myself yet to have taken hold of it. But one thing I do: Forgetting what is behind and straining toward what is ahead, I press on toward the goal to win the prize for which GOD has called me heavenward in CHRIST JESUS. All of us who are mature should take such a view of things. And if on some point, you think differently, that too GOD will make clear to you. Only let us live up to what we have already attained.

Philippians 3:12-16 NIV

CHAPTER FIVE

The Wait

I believe God is managing affairs and that
He doesn't need any advice from me.
With God in charge, I believe everything
will work out for the best in the end.
So what is there to worry about.
—Henry Ford (1863-1947)

Let nothing disturb thee;
Let nothing dismay thee;
All things pass; God never changes.
Patience attains All that it strives for;
He who has God finds he lacks nothing;
—Author Unknown

Many people have a strong aversion to waiting. Long lines at super discount stores, airport security check points and driver's license renewal offices all help to establish the negative impression of people lined up like mindless cattle unpleasantly waiting.

Have you ever arrived fifteen minutes early for a doctor or dentist visit only to wait at least thirty minutes beyond your scheduled appointment? Doesn't that burn you up—especially if you had to wait to get the appointment? What about a trip to a hair salon or a trip to a bank on a Friday afternoon. These times seem to test your patience beyond all limits.

Did you ever schedule an outing with someone where you were not the driver? This may have been an occasion that you were looking forward to with high hopes. Perhaps you take special care with your grooming and attire for this outing. You may even spend a considerable amount of time in mental preparation setting the mood for an enjoyable event.

Although you are ready at the appointed time, the driver is late and has not called to give you a new estimated time of arrival. Waiting for the inconsiderate driver could alter your pleasant mood. As more time ticks by, you may find yourself pacing and anxiously checking the windows every few moments.

After your tardy friend has missed the scheduled meeting by thirty minutes without calling, you may begin to assume the worst. Scenes of mechanical malfunctions or horrible car accidents may begin to run across your mind.

If your friend is habitually tardy, your emotions turn to anger as you berate yourself for expecting a different outcome this time. However, if your friend is usually a punctual person, you may second-guess your agreement. You may mentally replay your last conversation with him or her and wonder if perhaps you mistook the time.

No matter, when the hapless friend shows up over an hour late, *(Without calling, mind you!)* all types of negative emotions surface. You rediscover that you hate to wait! Here we go again, confined to the "**DRY PLACES**." When waiting for people, there is always a teensy bit of fear and suspicion that the long anticipated arrival of a person might not happen. The fear of disappointment is part of the reason for anxiety caused by waiting. A bad attitude produced by waiting anxiety can zoom us immediately to the **"DRY PLACES"** and could extend our stay there.

These bad attitudes are totally unacceptable when waiting for a promise of GOD to manifest. Waiting for the LORD should be undertaken with joy and confident hopefulness. GOD is not a man that HE should lie, if HE promises it shall surely happen. Waiting on GOD requires faith, trust, and absolute obedience.

Consider Abram who later had his name changed to Abraham by GOD. Abraham had so much faith that he obeyed GOD when told to go to a land he had never seen. His faith so pleased GOD that he was called *"friend"* by GOD. That term friend was not used lightly; rather it had all of the loving endearment and sincere affection that only GOD gives.

Starting at the twelfth chapter, of Genesis, Abram was a mere *seventy-five years young* when GOD appeared to him. Abram was instructed to take his wife and leave his extended family. GOD first promised at this point to make Abram a great nation. *"And I will make of you a great nation, and I will bless you [with abundant increase of favors] and make your name famous and distinguished, and you will be a blessing [dispensing good to others]. And I will bless those who bless you [who confer prosperity or happiness upon you] and[1] curse him who curses or uses insolent language toward you; in you will all the families and kindred of the earth be blessed [and by you they will bless themselves]. So Abram departed, as the LORD had directed him; and Lot [his nephew] went with him. Abram was seventy-five years old when he left Haran.* (Verses 12-4 AMP)

Next, we pick up another visitation to Abram sent from GOD one night in chapter fifteen, verse one. *After these things, the word of the LORD came to Abram in a vision, saying, Fear not, Abram, I am your Shield, your abundant compensation, and your reward shall be exceedingly great.*

In the subsequent verses, we read about a dialogue Abram had with GOD, his friend. While Abram was thankful that GOD was with him and would make him a great nation, he was sad that his wife was barren and had not borne any children. Abram felt that without an heir, all that he had amassed would be inherited by some one other than his direct lineage.

GOD took Abram outside and instructed him to look up at the starry sky. GOD told him to count the stars in the sky because that was how many descendents that would spring from HIS own body. GOD sealed his promise with a sacrifice that HE instructed Abram to make. Abraham's revelation of GOD'S ability was expanded and he was confident that GOD would bless him with a child from his very own body.

Do not become impatient when GOD gives you a promise in HIS Holy Word. From the time the oath is given to us, our hearts should be confident that GOD will do just what HE says without our interference. Occupy or remain productive until HE comes is a phrase that means that there are things we should be doing while we wait. To paraphrase a popular television evangelist, "If you are waiting for instructions from GOD, "Do what HE told you to do the last time HE spoke!" In other words when you do not know what else to do, keep doing what you know to do. Continue with those instructions no matter how long it takes.

When we pick up the story of Abram again in chapter sixteen, impatience has set in. Abram's wife Sarai persuades him to conceive a child with Hagar her handmaiden. Even though Sarai was not there when GOD spoke to Abram about the magnificent promise, she anxiously insisted upon a child immediately. Abram complied with his wife's suggestion and was eighty-six when his son with Hagar was born. Eleven years had transpired since the promise was given.

The wait was not over. Fourteen years later when Abram was ninety-nine, GOD visited him again. GOD established HIS covenant with Abram and changed his name to Abraham, father of many nations. As a sign of GOD'S covenant, Abraham was circumcised along with his entire household. GOD reminded Abraham that a son would be born to him through his wife. GOD even changed Sarai's name to Sarah, mother of many. Every time that Sarah and Abraham spoke to each other, they verbally reinforced GOD'S promise.

The following year, when Abraham reached one hundred years old, his son was born. Sarah was well past childbearing age and natural human functions had ceased! Both she and Abraham were considered old for new parents. Yet, Isaac was born according to the promise. The LORD visited Sarah in mercy, as HE had said. Isaac was born at the set time that GOD had spoken. No matter how impatient or agitated we may become, GOD is always punctual to HIS time. HIS promised mercies come not at the time people set, but they will certainly come at the time HE sets. Because we love and trust GOD, we know that GOD'S time is always the best time for us.

Sometimes blessings will come our way because we are in the right place at the right time. Our appointment with destiny can be connected to others around us. In chapter twenty-three, we read that Sarah died and later in chapter twenty-five Abraham married a second time and had more sons.

Keturah, Abraham's second wife was not mentioned in the Bible when GOD first made the promise. Many years had transpired and many things had happened before she came on the scene. Do you think her marriage and subsequent sons were a surprise to GOD?

When GOD makes us a promise, HE will fulfill it. Three women were used to fulfill GOD'S promise to Abraham. All were connected to him and reaped the benefits of GOD'S promise. Do not forfeit your blessings by trying to second-guess GOD. When you wait, know that GOD has a specific plan for your life. Think pleasant and uplifting thoughts as you wait. *Your Best Life Now* by Joel Osteen employs a great quote. "When you think positive, excellent thoughts, you will be propelled toward greatness."

Allow GOD to have HIS perfect will in your life. Wait, and keep waiting until GOD births from you the thing that pleases HIM. Submit yourself graciously unto the LORD, satisfied that HE wants only the best for you. In your patience, you will possess your soul. (Paraphrased Luke 21:19)

Your stay in the "**DRY PLACES**" will be shortened because you know the scripture promises in the Bible. GOD has granted the privilege of loosing, setting free, or causing to flow the things we want for our lives. No matter the trouble or situation, the answer is to find the scripture that supports our requests and let it loose! According to the Bible, if we remain in CHRIST and HIS words remain in us, we can ask whatever we wish, and it will be given to us. There is nothing too hard for GOD.

Realize that it is not GOD'S will for you to allow your wait to be a dry, anxious time. You will soar like an eagle high above naysayers and dream killers. You will be established firmly in the destiny tailor made just for you. Keep evolving and allow your hope within to grow bigger and spread larger!

But those who wait on the LORD shall renew their strength; they shall mount up with wings like eagles, they shall run and not be weary, they shall walk and not faint. Isaiah 40:31 NKJV

Heavenly FATHER,

*Thank YOU, Thank YOU, Thank YOU.
I purpose now to wait patiently for
YOUR manifested greatness in my life.
I look around me and see all of the wonderful things
YOU are doing for me and no longer feel the need to hurry,
rush or speed through my life with YOU.
I thank YOU for teaching me to wait graciously
for YOUR direction. While waiting for specific instructions,
I choose to spend my time in prayer, studying YOUR word
and serving others in the body of CHRIST.
In the precious name of JESUS, I pray,*

Amen.

CHAPTER SIX

The Servant/Leader

*"The first responsibility of a leader
is to define reality.
The last is to say thank you.
In between, the leader is a servant."
—Max De Pree, "Leadership Is an Art"*

*Leadership is action, not position.
—Donald H. McGannon*

*A leader leads by example,
whether he intends to or not.
—Anonymous*

Serving GOD is the ultimate objective of a servant leader. A servant leader is a person who desires to lead or excel in serving GOD.

The dictionary defines a servant as one who serves. A servant is the person who works for someone else's comfort or assists in meeting another person's needs. Commonly, a servant is so usable that often their service brings about very low or menial compensation. Many view servants as people of low intelligence with no personal lives. Often servants are underappreciated, taken for granted and treated with very little respect or dignity.

Sometimes the word servant is synonymous with the word slave and is used interchangeably. The general portrayal is a person in bondage and subjugation as property of another. Hard work and cruel drudgery completes the imagery of slavery and servant-hood. The concept has been so maligned that being a servant or slave is the very last thing a person would aspire to become. Most people cringe at the very idea of becoming a servant to an idea, *(Servant to social standing)* or an emotion *(Slave to love)* because it reinforces the implication of forced homage and a lack of free will.

The world views a servant as the lowest position on the totem pole or the very least person in the pecking order. While the world's primary objective is to be exalted to lofty heights, the true servant has the more humble aspiration of being pleasing in the sight of Almighty GOD. The world cannot grasp the concept that JESUS taught about the servant being the greatest among the group. That very idea is diametrically opposed to the world's viewpoint. **(Aren't you glad GOD does not have a Pecking Order and has banished that barbaric practice to the barnyard where it belongs?)**

On the other hand, the term leader conveys the sense of one being on the very top. The leader excels far beyond the norm, is above average and is the person who makes things happen while motivating others to follow. It is exciting just being around a leader.

Leaders are thought of as the people calling the shots, the ones in charge, the head honchos and are the ones that far out distance the rest. Most people want to cultivate their leadership abilities and consider it a compliment when leadership traits are recognized in them. Even people who pride themselves in being behind the scenes types just love to be recognized as content in the background while they quarterback or lead from the sidelines.

The dictionary defines a leader as one who guides, conducts, escorts or directs. A leader influences, induces and is ahead in the front position. They are called upon to take risks and meet opposition head on. They cannot shirk responsibility nor run away from challenges. Leaders are considered the chiefs who encourage a desired response. The world sees leaders as the large and in charge types who take control.

Leaders are people who are examples and can be role models for others to follow. In academia, the intellectual leader is the person others can depend on for the answers. In sports, the leading world-class athlete in a particular event sets the standard for the team to meet or beat. In an orchestra, the lead instrumentalist within a section is the one the others try to emulate while playing their parts. In chaotic situations, panicking people look to the leaders to restore order and give directions.

In every instance, leadership requires discipline, diligence and determination. Leaders recognize the importance of his or her role and see the gravity of their actions. Leaders are not shallow, are willing to step up to center stage and will put his or her entire being in what they are doing.

However, trying to merge the characteristics of a servant with a leader can send well-meaning people shrieking to the "**DRY PLACES.**" Sharing natural gifts of leadership within some group dynamics can cause conflicts. If natural leadership abilities are not nurtured, the leader will feel boxed in and chained to the "**DRY PLACES.**" It is the enemy's objective to hold back plus keep down GOD'S people and unfruitful people are the best candidates to accomplish it. Unproductive people are often lazy and are not really living up to their full potential. They believe that by thwarting the real leaders, their inactivity will be excused. *(Don't they know GOD sees?)*

Even with individuals who desire to serve, the "**DRY PLACES**" makes them feel used up, wrung out dry, unappreciated and taken for granted. If these emotions do not overwhelm them, they become convinced that someone else is smarter, more talented and better equipped for the task.

If he or she runs into the opposition of turf protectors, they will retreat to prevent conflict. *(Help LORD JESUS!)*

The story of Nehemiah is a good example of someone who learned to combine the attributes of both a servant and leader. Nehemiah was in exile in Susa, a Persian city. He was a servant to the king as the royal cupbearer. Nehemiah heard about all of the trouble miles away in his home country of Judah and the deplorable living conditions. He thought it disgraceful that the walls of the city had burned years earlier in battle and had not been rebuilt.

Nehemiah was so saddened that he sat down and wept. He fasted for several days and prayed. In Nehemiah's prayer, he acknowledged the disobedience of his people and the deserved judgment of GOD. His prayer asked for mercy on behalf of his people and specifically asked for GOD'S intervention with the King. *O LORD, please hear my prayer! Heed the prayers of those of us who delight to honor you. Please help me now as I go in and ask the king for a great favor-put it into his heart to be kind to me."* Nehemiah 1:11 TLB

Several months later when Nehemiah was serving the King's wine, his face was sad. The king noticed and asked Nehemiah what was the matter. Interesting note; Nehemiah was a servant in the presence of royalty. It was customary for servants to appear jovial and grateful to serve in the King's inner circle. Usually servants are invisible to their masters. It was remarkable that the King noticed and that he cared enough to ask questions.

With a quick prayer to the GOD of heaven, I replied, "If it please Your Majesty and if you look upon me with your royal favor, send me to Judah to rebuild the city of my fathers!" Nehemiah 2:4 TLB. With GOD on his side, Nehemiah was bold enough to respond to the king. The king agreed to let him go as requested and asked for an estimate for the amount of time it would take to complete his task. *(In other words, the king granted him a leave of absence from service.)*

Nehemiah reached an agreement with the king and asked for royal letters to carry as he traveled through neighboring countries. He also asked for timber to use building the gates and a personal residence. GOD softened the heart of the king who did all that Nehemiah asked. The king also sent army officers and cavalry troops to escort Nehemiah safely to Judah.

In the midst of GOD'S amazing blessings to Nehemiah and his people, jealousy was stirred up in the hearts of leading officials in neighboring countries. Jealousy is so ugly in anyone that it stirs up rage, malice and hatred. For the nearby countries, the very thought that the people of Israel were getting help made the rulers burn with resentment.

After arriving in the city of Jerusalem, Nehemiah went out at night surveying the condition of the burnt and crumbled walls of the city. None of the city officials, priests or other countrymen knew what Nehemiah had in mind. Nehemiah simply observed what needed to be done.

When Nehemiah went to the leaders later, he wisely remarked about the condition of the ruined walls and suggested that they all work together to rebuild them. Nehemiah shared with them all of the wonderful things that had been granted by the king. *(There is a tactful way to enlist the help of others!)* The people agreed to begin work immediately. Sometimes when others know what needs to be done, they are waiting for a leader to emerge and motivate them to do it.

When envious neighboring leaders heard about the repair plans, they were so filled with spite that they began to ridicule and insult the workers. They falsely accused Nehemiah of rebelling against the king. Nehemiah was not afraid to answer the vicious rumors against him. He knew that as servants of The Most High GOD, the work would succeed. He also knew that it was none of their business, and his antagonist had no part in what GOD wanted done.

The people joined together by families and worked on various parts of the city wall simultaneously. While the people worked hard, they endured the taunts and ill-will of their neighboring enemies. Again, Nehemiah prayed. He told GOD about the hostility and loathing that spewed forth from their enemies. Nehemiah asked GOD to allow all of the mean and horrible things wished upon the builders to fall back on the heads of their enemies.

The walls were half way up when the enemies became more vicious. The builders continued to pray and work and they posted guards around the clock. The people on the outskirts of the city warned of surprise attacks at least ten times. Nehemiah encouraged the workers and told them to fight for their relatives, children, wives and homes.

When the cowardly enemies discovered that the builders knew about their plots and were prepared to fight, they backed down. GOD had again been gracious to Nehemiah and the people by preventing the enemies' schemes from succeeding. *(**What a mighty GOD we serve**)* When you are serving the LORD and danger arises, GOD will move you out of harm's way. No matter how many mean spirited people connive to harm you, greater is GOD who is on your side.

After the foiled attempt to attack the builders, Nehemiah had half of the men work while the other half stood guard. The workers also strapped on swords and were prepared to defend themselves. With the workers spread out over a large area, they decided that wherever the trumpet sounded everyone would quickly gather to fight off marauding enemies.

Day by day from dawn to dark, half of the workers rebuilt the walls, while the rest stood guard with spears. The workers slept in their work clothes with weapons close by. Those dedicated servants had to work under extreme conditions. The focus was on getting the job done rather on personal comfort.

One of the tricks used to stop the work of the LORD is internal strife. If seeds of discord can be planted from within a previously unified group, complaints get overblown. Disagreements arise and harsh words are spoken. Ultimately, the work stops or is delayed.

Within Nehemiah's camp of workers, a dispute arose. The officials and leaders of the nation were charging their fellow countrymen interest and selling them into slavery. Nehemiah became angry and appealed to the leaders to live their lives in ways that would honor GOD. Instead of giving food and grain expecting to be repaid at an exorbitant rate, Nehemiah asked them to share with one another freely. Nehemiah refused to be a burden on the people for the time he spent rebuilding the wall. He did not ask them for a food allowance, but instead looked to GOD for his blessings. *(**Leading by example**)* Despite the dispute, the work continued.

When the enemies discovered that the city walls had been completely rebuilt except for the doors, they conspired again to harm Nehemiah. They invited Nehemiah to meet with them on four separate occasions. Each time Nehemiah refused saying that his work was too important to slow down or stop for a visit with them. Nehemiah was intent upon finishing what he had started.

An insidious rumor was launched to frighten Nehemiah and keep him from completing his task. ***(Your enemies will stoop to the lowest levels to stop you!)*** Again, Nehemiah prayed and asked GOD for strength. The dastardly enemies went so low as to pay a false prophet hoping it would entice Nehemiah to run for his life and hide in the temple. Yet GOD was Nehemiah's constant source of confidence throughout the entire building project.

When the neighboring enemies discovered that the work was finally finished, they felt helpless because they knew GOD was on the side of Nehemiah and his people. When GOD opens a door, no man can shut it. When GOD wants things done, HE will supernaturally move obstacles out of our way. All HE requires of us is to remain faithful and focused on our assignment.

Nehemiah was in the perfect place to emerge as a leader and to undertake this assignment from GOD. He was in exile serving in the background of the royal court. The period spent as a servant uniquely qualified Nehemiah to lead because he learned to submit to authority. When the time came, GOD elevated Nehemiah and removed him from the place of his forced servitude.

Often times when GOD wants to use you or me in a leadership capacity, HE spends time grooming us with humility, compassion and perseverance. When GOD calls and gives spiritual gifts, it is for the use of the entire body of CHRIST. Believers are uniquely endowed by the HOLY SPIRIT to make a positive impact in the world around them. This is not a gift that evil people can stop, block or prevent. When yielded to GOD, HE will cause HIS plans to succeed!

The "**DRY PLACES**" are merely portions of the enemy's tricks and devices to stop our forward progress in CHRIST. As Nehemiah experienced, the enemy will try all types of low down dirty tricks to frustrate us. We can start to focus on the evil ploys rather than the task ahead for us and become mired down in the "**DRY PLACES**." Throughout our lives it is no doubt that, we will visit the "**DRY PLACES**." ***(Often against our will)*** It is up to us though how long we stay there.

Recently, while dining at a five star restaurant, I received superior service. From fresh ground pepper for my salad or a special sauce to compliment my meat selection, each time I thanked my waiter, he always replied, "My Pleasure!" The waiter's expression, demeanor and gracious attention to detail heighten my dining experience. It brought a smile to my face and I thoroughly enjoyed myself. Guess what. That waiter got a large tip! Like the waiter, it is my pleasure to serve the LORD. I will sing unto HIM because I am filled with Joy! The great tip I receive is the knowledge that my service, praise and worship makes GOD smile and I will spend eternity in HIS presence.

When things become unbearable and threaten to stop us, we must each decide to lay aside every weight the "**DRY PLACES**" puts in our way and press on. Never stop even if you feel too weak to go on another day. The source of your strength is the joy of the LORD that cannot be taken away from you. Dig in and press with all of your might. Like JESUS, we must be about the FATHER'S business. Get out of the "**DRY PLACES**" and do what GOD has called you to do! Learn the lessons of humility and kindness. Grow in your commitment of excellence in everything you do. Serve GOD by leading and lead by serving. Do not shrink back from what GOD has planned for you. Even if it means taking tiny baby steps, keep moving forward. There is still much to accomplish!

Dear Heavenly FATHER,

*It is my pleasure to serve YOU and
I thank YOU for the privilege.
No matter how it may look to others, I know
that to humbly serve YOU is the greatest honor of all.
YOUR word promises that my gifts will make room
for me so I am determined to stir up the gifts
YOU have given me. I will not neglect them.
Help me to lead others to a relationship with YOU.
I want to be a leader in sharing my faith and
showing forth YOUR love to others.
In the precious name of JESUS, I pray,*

Amen.

CHAPTER SEVEN

The Aged

*It is never too late to be
who you might have been.*
—George Elliot

*A man is not old until regrets
start taking place of dreams.*
—Anonymous

*Dreams are renewable.
No matter what our age or condition,
there are still untapped possibilities within us
and new beauty waiting to be born.*
—Dr. Dale Turner

"**O**LD! You are OLD!"

"What do you mean OLD? I'm not OLD"

"Yes you are. You are old!"

Ever have this argument with the person in your mirror? Have you ever noticed crow's feet around your eyes, a gray hair or an age spot and feel like crying?

The "**DRY PLACES**" try to sentence many souls to a permanent residence *(Without a nice view)* with the notion that he or she is too old to be of any use in the kingdom of GOD. If you are over a certain age, the "**DRY PLACES**" taunt you with the notion that you are only in the way. The "**DRY PLACES**" want you to feel threatened by those who are younger.

The *certain age* is subjective and can be changed at the whim of whoever is in control. I can remember a time in life anyone over the age of thirty was considered old and an enemy to youth. People forty and beyond were called ancient, pre-historic and the crypt keepers! Corporate downsizing, job layoffs, aches, pains, and age related debilitating illnesses all create hostile environments for aging. Everyone wants to be perceived as young and still up with the latest lingo. No one wants to be called old! Many times adults will make embarrassing spectacles of themselves trying to have a bit of youthful fun. Rather than respect and appreciation for the experiences of the aged, our society *(Even in the church!)* holds such disdain and very little tolerance for those over the certain age.

Unfortunately, many have bought into this mindset never recognizing that GOD, the Ancient of Days, is in control. GOD sets the rules and determines who is still useful for the kingdom. GOD has even declared fifty as the year of jubilee and the age of *new beginnings*. As long as there is life in our bodies, how dare we set up permanent residence on rocking chairs in the "**DRY PLACES?**"

There are many instances recorded in the Bible where GOD used men and women after a certain age. Some of the aged people did extraordinary things at the point in life that others might be slowing down and retiring.

And Noah was six hundred years old when the flood of waters was upon the earth. Genesis 7:6 KJV

Noah had spent years building an ark according to GOD'S specification. The life he lived up to that point had been exemplary and GOD rewarded him with the provision to save himself and his household. The flood that was sent to destroy the earth was unprecedented and was designed to kill every living creature on the face of the earth. In the time when all humankind was living wicked and sinful lives, Noah was an example for all eternity. Holy Scripture encourages us to not become weary in doing what is right because in time we will be rewarded. No matter what everyone else is doing around us these days, we should be motivated to lift up a higher standard with our life style.

And Abraham was an hundred years old, when his son Isaac was born unto him. Genesis 21:5 KJV The remarkable thing about Abraham's age testimony is that in all of his years on earth, his first child was born to his wife's handmaiden at her suggestion. It speaks about fidelity, honor and integrity. Not only was Abraham's life pleasing to GOD, but also year after year, he honored his marriage vows. The very fact that Abraham told GOD that he did not have an heir says that he had not sought justification to stray away from his marriage covenant.

At that time, a man could lie with his wife and have concubines among her servants. The children produced from these encounters were considered a part of their master's lineage. Today, infertility is a major problem with a large number of couples. Fault-finding happens and causes some husbands and wives to forsake their marriage vows of fidelity. This passage however, should inspire couples to remain faithful in their marriage and to allow GOD to bless their union.

And Moses was eighty years old and Aaron eighty-three, when they spoke to Pharaoh. Exodus 7:7 NAS

Like Moses, a date with destiny could take years to prepare for. "*Winning Is Everything* by Rev. Roderick Zak illustrates the point that GOD humbled Moses to prepare him for a mighty work. It took years in exile for Moses to become very dependent on GOD. When GOD first encountered Moses with instructions concerning his task, Moses was afraid. Moses did not think he could do it. He made excuses. Moses was at a point that he was enjoying his life as a simple goat herder far away from his earlier years. It was a safe existence with very little risk.

It does not matter how long we have been away or how old we are when GOD calls. HE is able to equip us and sustain us to get the job done. We should never be afraid to do what GOD compels us to do. Where GOD guides, HE will provide and sometimes that provision is you and your willingness to obey.

Caleb and Joshua were mighty warriors before the LORD and were both used in many victories. Caleb's testimony is recorded; *"And now behold, the LORD has let me live, just as He spoke, these forty-five years, from the time that the LORD spoke this word to Moses, when Israel walked in the wilderness; and now behold, I am eighty-five years old today. I am still as strong today as I was in the day Moses sent me; as my strength was then, so my strength is now, for war and for going out and coming in.* Joshua 14:10-11 NAS

One of the women I like to read about is Anna the Prophetess. She dedicated many decades of her life in total service in GOD'S temple. She had lived seven years with a husband, yet after being widowed, she gave the rest of her life to GOD. Those years were not wasted because most religious art portrays her holding baby JESUS at the temple. It gave Anna great pleasure to be an eyewitness of JESUS' actual presence in the world.

And there was a prophetess, Anna the daughter of Phanuel, of the tribe of Asher. She was advanced in years, having lived with a husband seven years after her marriage, and then as a widow to the age of eighty-four. And she never left the temple, serving night and day with fastings and prayers. And at that very moment she came up and began giving thanks to GOD, and continued to speak of Him to all those who were looking for the redemption of Jerusalem. Luke 3:35-38 NAS

There is also purpose for old age that the Bible teaches in the second chapter of Titus. Older men are to be temperate, dignified, sensible, sound in faith, in love, in perseverance. In other words, the fruits of the spirit should be evident in the way they conduct themselves. **(Love, joy, peace, patience, kindness, goodness, faithfulness, gentleness and self-control)**

Older men become the mentors for younger men. Far and large, most churches have more women members than men. Somehow serving GOD has gotten a bad rap and is perceived as a feminine undertaking. Men have been so conditioned to camouflage their emotions, that open adoration of the LORD is discouraged. With strong, manly men properly modeling worship and service to our Omnipotent GOD, other men will feel free to participate.

In addition, older women are to set positive examples by their behavior. They should not be malicious gossips; rather older women should teach what is good. These women have the experience to encourage the young women to love their husbands and their children. Often when trying to live day by day it may appear that family life can be too demanding and difficult to handle. This is where first hand experience comes in. The women who can share their experiences have a lot more credibility than someone spouting what they recently read by the latest self-help guru.

Sometimes it takes common sense observations sprinkled with experience to offer strategies for dealing with an unruly child or wayward husband. What might seem earth shattering in our youth becomes another one of life's challenges to the aged. The Bible urges you to make every effort to produce a life of moral excellence. *A life of moral excellence leads to knowing GOD better. Knowing GOD leads to self-control. Self-control leads to patient endurance, and patient endurance leads to godliness. Godliness leads to love for other Christians, and finally you will grow to have genuine love for everyone. The more you grow like this, the more you will become productive and useful in your knowledge of our Lord Jesus Christ.* (2 Peter 15-7 NLT) With age and experience come mellowness, calm and fewer bouts of frantic energy. Witnessing GOD'S supernatural move to bless what seemed impossible before, gives the seasoned woman the confidence that GOD will move on her behalf again.

Many times when you see a younger person doing something that experience has taught you will bring a disastrous outcome, do you keep silent? If so, why? Are you afraid that you may appear old and not with it? Have you been told to relax and loosen up? It is always good advice to relax and to loosen up, but do not allow those words to keep you from offering assistance when you see trouble ahead. Sometimes your vantage point is the only clear view of the upcoming dangerous pitfall!

If you ever had the unpleasant task of issuing a warning of danger that went unheeded, you may be tempted to clam up and never, ever help again! Resist that urge and continue to gently share in truth and love. If one out of ten people ever thank you, you are in good company. **(Remember JESUS and the ten lepers!)** No one wants to be labeled a nag. Neither would anyone want to live with the guilt of seeing someone suffer needlessly because the alarms **(In your control)** were not sounded.

There are things GOD has purposed for you to accomplish in your lifetime. It will be rewarding and fulfilling for you. Do not quit and give up now. Never allow the enemy to persuade you to sit on the sidelines missing your blessings. Do not let the enemy keep you stuck in the "**DRY PLACES**" pining for the good ole days. Press and Push! Keep at it and do no give up!

There is a deep hunger in each of us to feel needed, wanted, and accepted. Strong relationships thrive on the fact that each person needs the other. Enduring marriages seem to have the common thread that couples give the impression that they complete each other. One person's strengths and weaknesses are complimented by those of his or her spouse. While each can accomplish nice things, it appears that greater things are done when they work together.

Embrace where you are in life with GOD. Thank GOD, that things are as well as they are. You are alive; therefore, you must not stop growing. Because JESUS lives, you can face your tomorrow. Longevity is a tremendous blessing granted to you by GOD. Enjoy it! The body of CHRIST can still benefit from your experiences and the valuable lessons you have learned.

Get out of the "**DRY PLACES.**" You are not too old. GOD still wants you to do the things HE has appointed for your life. The place GOD has for you is secure and no one else can block it! The lessons you have mastered are needed in the kingdom, still.

Dear Heavenly FATHER,

*Please help me to continue to
live a life that is pleasing unto YOU.
Even when the enemy tries to whisper that,
I am too old or that someone else is too old to work
in service unto the LORD, help me to get rid of that notion.
I know that if I abide with YOU that I will remain fruitful.
Each year, I want to get sweeter and sweeter.
I present my body a living sacrifice unto YOU.
In the name of JESUS, I pray,*

Amen.

STOP

*TAKE A
PRAISE
BREAK!*

When you consider how many years, GOD protected you, begin to thank and praise HIM!

- ✓ *PRAISE GOD FOR CALLING YOU HIS FRIEND!*

- ✓ *PRAISE GOD FOR HIS EVERLASTING LOVE TOWARDS YOU!*

- ✓ *PRAISE GOD FOR THE WONDERFUL PLANS HE HAS FOR YOUR LIFE!*

CHAPTER EIGHT

The Pass Code

Desire, ask, believe, receive.
—*Stella Terrill Mann*

*Vision without action is a daydream.
Action without vision is a nightmare.*
—*Japanese Proverb*

*Never discourage anyone . . . who continually
makes progress, no matter how slow.*
—*Plato*

Get Out Of The "DRY PLACES"

One of the things that many super heroes have in common is a password or pass code that they can use to signal that they are in deep trouble and need help. Most of the time, in a super hero saga, things can look so bad, that there appears to be no escape.

Maybe the hero becomes outnumbered and surrounded by a group of menacing foes. Perhaps the hero would be beat down to an extremely weaken state bleeding from what looks like mortal injuries. Sometimes the hero would have onlookers who offered no assistance and scoffed at the mere idea of victory on the hero's part.

Just speaking the pass code aloud with a strong and confident voice would somehow summon unseen help from out of thin air! The hero would defeat the foes, amaze the skeptics, and receive the victory.

Even in our day-to-day existence, pass codes are needed. To gain access to the ATM, to check voice mail and to read our E-mails, pass codes are required. Pass codes are used to protect our privacy and to secure property. To operate some vehicles, you must enter a pass code just to get in the driver's seat.

Employers give out pass codes to their employees to grant entry to secure places within the organization. Their employees are expected to use these pass codes as needed to perform their assigned duties. Excuses for not having the pass code are unacceptable and usually to replace a lost pass code can be costly and inconvenient.

This analogy helps to define our position within the kingdom of GOD. We each have been given a pass code at the time of our redemption. The pass code is to be used in completing our assignments here on earth. Instructions on how to use the pass code have been left in the Bible. Each person is expected to become familiar with the instructions and to apply them in his or her daily life.

So many are trapped in the "**DRY PLACES**" because they cannot seem to put their fingers on what it is they need and why their lives seem so dry and empty. Too often persons in these positions find little enjoyment in worshipping and praising GOD. With these folks, personal relationships are in shambles and daily life seems pointless.

The "**DRY PLACES**" have these types of people stuck in the very core where all sides seem to be closing in on them. People who remain in this state can stay there until all of the life has been sucked out of them. They will become so shriveled and dried up that they can crumble away to nothingness.

Usually dried up people can't stand the fresh joy found in others outside of the "**DRY PLACES**." They often envy the peace and anointing that surrounds blessed people. Those without the pass code do not spend their energies on trying to escape the "**DRY PLACES**," instead; they will attempt to drag others there too.

To escape these "**DRY PLACES**" require people to press with all of their might. Like when trying to wake oneself up from a terrifying nightmare, this requires effort on our part. The pass code that we each should use to escape the "**DRY PLACES**" is the name of JESUS.

There is salvation in the name of JESUS. Whether male or female, each person has the opportunity to accept JESUS CHRIST as his or her personal savior to receive deliverance from an eternity of being separated from GOD. It is a great mystery how merely submitting to GOD'S way of doing things bring about salvation and redemption. That submission is the acknowledgement that we need JESUS and are doomed sinners without HIM. We make the decision to repent from a previous lifestyle without JESUS and allow HIS grace and mercy to give us a regenerated and loving heart.

It is amazing, and too much for the natural mind to grasp how salvation is possible. Intellectuals might theorize that some lofty and noteworthy action must be undertaken to be granted this precious gift. It is difficult for cerebral types to simplify the process. Salvation is awarded through faith in JESUS and not a great deed done by people. It is not awarded by brilliant or lofty deduction. If that were the case, only people with extremely high IQ's could obtain it. Salvation is not acquired by paying a great sum of money. If that were so, only very rich people could afford it.

Salvation is not reserved only for talented, attractive, athletic, young, old or popular people. It is not only for a special race, nationality or gender. Salvation is available to everyone who believes and accepts JESUS CHRIST as LORD of all. Salvation is to recognize that your life is headed in the wrong direction. Stop! Turn Around! Ask for GOD'S forgiveness. Realize that you cannot make it without JESUS CHRIST. Accept HIM in your heart as your LORD and SAVIOR. Allow the love of CHRIST to make you brand new.

Our access to the throne of grace and the holy of holies is with the pass code; the name of JESUS. *And everyone who calls on the name of the LORD will be saved.'* Acts 2:21 NIV JESUS instructed in the fourteenth chapter of John *"And I will do whatever you ask in my name, so that the Son may bring glory to the Father. You may ask me for anything in my name, and I will do it."* (Verses 13&14)NIV

This provision is like receiving a blank check or a platinum credit card. We have been authorized to make the expenditures because JESUS has already paid the bill. The very fact that the pass code is in the name of JESUS keeps you and me from making foolish or evil request. The name of JESUS is so powerful that it purifies our prayerful request. We might intend to make a greedy request, but as soon as it is sealed with the name of JESUS, our hearts become convicted to submit to HIS holy will. With the name of JESUS as the pass code that has been freely given to us, we are inspired to live up to a high standard of integrity. Not to sully the name becomes a sincere desire on our part.

The sixteenth chapter of Mark tells of another advantage Christians have in the name of JESUS. *"And these attesting signs will accompany those who believe: in MY name they will drive out demons; they will speak in new languages; They will pick up serpents; and [even] if they drink anything deadly, it will not hurt them; they will lay their hands on the sick, and they will get well."* (Verses 17&18) AMP

Just think, the name of JESUS is so healing that things that could normally be deadly are rendered powerless! This pass code is ours to use when sickness prolongs our stay in the **"DRY PLACES."** Case after case of miraculous healings are recorded in the Bible during the earthly ministry of JESUS CHRIST. HE was always moved with compassion to relieve the suffering and cure deadly diseases within the masses. The only prerequisite was faith on the part of the injured. It is still GOD'S desire that we all live healthy, abundant and prosperous lives.

The name of JESUS is the anecdote when suddenly calamity occurs of a demonic source. The very fact that the provision is given for help against demons is proof that spiritual warfare does happen.

The Three Battlefields by Francis Frangipane looks at spiritual warfare in the mind, church and the heavenly places. The warfare in the mind is a dimension to the human nature that can host an evil spirit. The warfare in the church uses division and strife to pit Christians against one another. The warfare in heavenly places involves the unholy influences prevalent in our society, country and entire world. It is so good to know that our pass code, the name of JESUS, cancels and defeats the demonic intentions of the enemy. The disciples who had been sent out as witnesses exclaimed with joy, *"LORD, even the demons submit to us in your name."* Luke 10:17 NIV

There are miracles imbedded in the name of JESUS, just waiting for someone bold enough to say the name. A miracle is a wonderful happening beyond the known laws of nature. It is something marvelous that has been accomplished unusually despite extreme difficulties or impossible situations. The realm of the impossible becomes possible.

Manifesting the miraculous requires bold faith while accessing the name of JESUS. It is refusing to follow the crowd with the belief that something is a lost cause without remedy. It requires knowing that you have the pass code to take everything to JESUS. Like the lyrics to popular praise songs, "There's something about that name! JESUS is the sweetest name I know." Then Peter said, *"Silver or gold I do not have, but what I have I give you. In the name of JESUS CHRIST of Nazareth, walk."* Acts 16:6 NIV

The Bible gives the account of a testimony Paul and Silas experienced as they invoked the name of JESUS. "Once when we were going to the place of prayer, we were met by a slave girl who had a spirit by which she predicted the future. She earned a great deal of money for her owners by fortune telling. This girl followed Paul and the rest of us, shouting, "These men are servants of the Most High GOD, who are telling you the way to be saved." She kept this up for many days. Finally, Paul became so troubled that he turned around and said to the spirit, *"In the name of JESUS CHRIST I command you to come out of her!"* At that moment the spirit left her." Acts 16:16-18 NIV

The pass code had authority over other spirits! This passage helps to clear up any confusion anyone might have about the potency of the name of JESUS. Sometimes when encountering someone in authority or of great influence, fear and trepidation can rock our confidence. This trepidation could lock us into the **"DRY PLACES"** afraid to move forward in our purpose. This earthly authority may try to block our progress on every side, but we have been appointed and anointed by GOD for a place of greatness.

Regardless of every scheme devised by unscrupulous people, "greater is HE that is within us than he that is in the world." At the very name of JESUS, everything trying to ensnare us has to let go! The **"DRY PLACES"** do not have authority and power over us. Hallelujah!

"Therefore GOD exalted Him to the highest place and gave Him the name that is above every name, that at the name of JESUS every knee should bow, in heaven and on earth and under the earth, and every tongue confess that JESUS CHRIST is LORD," Phil 2:9-11 NIV

The pass code out of the **"DRY PLACES"** should be used constantly. By proclaiming the power in the name of JESUS, we can change the atmosphere around us. Instead of being held captive in the **"DRY PLACES,"** we are set free. There is freedom wherever the spirit of the LORD is present.

The HOLY SPIRIT actually does the bidding that the pass code releases. HE is the third person of the Godhead and is present wherever JESUS is. Without the power of the HOLY SPIRIT, sent by the FATHER and given through JESUS CHRIST, we are living beneath our privilege in GOD. The **"DRY PLACES"** cannot contain the HOLY SPIRIT. The very nature of the HOLY SPIRIT brings light and is lively. Anything unholy and unpleasant is rendered powerless and insignificant. Regardless of outward conditions, with JESUS, you are blessed, fortunate, and spiritually prosperous.

The **"DRY PLACES"** are not home to anyone. Once you recognize it, renounce it. Pack up your hope and dreams and use your pass code to get out of there!

Dear JESUS,

*I love YOU! I thank YOU for dying
on the cross for me. I give up any form of
rebellion and sin in my life and I commit to
live my life according to YOUR purpose for me.
Please help me to boldly come against spiritual
wickedness and strongholds in my mind,
my church family and within the heavenly
places through the authority given in YOUR name.
Thank YOU for the precious gift of the HOLY SPIRIT.
Allow the anointing to saturate every thing that
I say and do for YOUR Glory.
It is in YOUR name JESUS, I pray,*

Amen.

PRAISE WORTHY

When I enter into the praise of our LORD, either alone or corporately, it is like being taken up to a high place in the LORD. High above everything and everyone around me. My heart becomes fixed on GOD and I am told that a heavenly glow can be seen on my face by others. So wrapped up in the radiance of the LORD, I can quickly make my way out of the "DRY PLACES!" Once you decide not to stay in "DRY PLACES," begin to Praise GOD, watch HIS riches blessings over take you, and transport you out!

> Know that the LORD is GOD. It is He, who made us, and
> we are His; we are His people, the sheep of His pasture.
> Enter His gates with thanksgiving and His courts with *praise;*
> give thanks to Him and *praise* His name.
> For the LORD is good and His love endures forever;
> His faithfulness continues through all generations.
> Ps 100:3-5 NIV

> Let everything that has breath *praise* the LORD.
> Praise the LORD.
> Ps 150:6 NIV

STOP

TAKE A

PRAISE

BREAK!

When you consider the wonderful relationships GOD has given you, begin to thank and praise HIM!

- ✓ *PRAISE GOD FOR THE EMPOWERMENT OF HIS HOLY SPIRIT!*

- ✓ *PRAISE GOD FOR VICTORY!*

- ✓ *PRAISE GOD FOR MAKING YOUR WAY PROSPEROUS.*

CHAPTER NINE

The Laughter

*"[Humanity] has unquestionably one
really effective weapon—laughter.
Power, money, persuasion, supplication,
persecution—these can lift at a colossal
humbug—push it a little—weaken it a little,
century by century; but only laughter can blow it
to rags and atoms at a blast. Against the assault
of laughter nothing can stand."*
—Mark Twain, The Mysterious Stranger, ch. 10, 1916

*To laugh often and much; to win the respect of
intelligent people and the affection of children;
to earn the appreciation of honest critics
and endure the betrayal of false friends;
to appreciate beauty, to find the best in others;
to leave the world a bit better,
whether by a healthy child, a garden patch
or a redeemed social condition;
to know even one life has breathed easier
because you have lived.
This is to have succeeded*
—Ralph Waldo Emerson

My son shared with me the abbreviations used to show amusement when sending an instant message e-mail. He told me ST means slightly tickled and LOL means laughing out loud. I began to use these acronyms, smiling each time I sent him an instant message.

It made me remember that once in an ethics class in college, my professor told the class that the immortals of Greek mythology had the ability to laugh in the midst of difficult circumstances. Somehow, the immortals knew that their merriment in the things that caused mere humans to fall apart, defied natural laws. They saw those things as merely temporary inconveniences. Their laughter released a confident assurance that not even unexpected ordeals can spoil their eternal existence.

When illustrations about angels are given, their mode of movement from one place to another is through astro-projection. These beings could merely speak a word or would think about it and were transported instantly to another place. Even in modern movie scenes, the recent "dearly departed" person would at break neck speed appear from one place to another. It was as if the human laws of time and space had no authority over them. All of the earthly rules and restrictions had been suspended.

All of these examples had the same thing in common. They all had the ability to do something considered impossible. It may be a mystery to some or Greek to others, but faith works a lot like that. Scripture assures us that, *"Now faith is the substance of things hoped for and the evidence of things not seen."* Hebrews 11:1 KJV. In other words, faith operates in a supernatural realm. It has the power to transport believers quickly to another place. It is faith in GOD that we utilize to move ourselves immediately from the **"DRY PLACES."**

It is our faith that can allow us to laugh out loud no matter what we face. It is that faith that reassures us that no matter what the test, GOD is able to bring us out rejoicing with praise. We can go through a traumatic time in life that frequently reduces us to tears. Yet with much prayer and daily pressing onward, GOD can turn our tears to spontaneous outbreaks of laughter.

If we look at the Bible story of Shadrach, Meshach and Abednego in the third chapter of Daniel, we can get a glimpse of a terrible injustice done to these three men at the hand of a wicked king. We know that these three young men were going about their task unaware of evil plots devised against them.

King Nebuchadnezzar had built a golden statue and placed it in a valley near the city of Babylon. A dedication ceremony took place and a royal decree was given. The king commanded musicians to play all sorts of instruments as a signal to call his subjects into an act of worship. The king decreed that at the sound of the music, every one was to bow down before the statue and worship it. The king further decreed that anyone who did not bow down and worship the statue would be thrown into a hot furnace and burned alive. The people, fearful for their lives obeyed. As soon as the music played, on cue the terrified people would bow down and worship the statue. What a sad state. Their worship was not genuine, merely motivated by fear. *(Hopefully, none of our worship is programmed just because music is playing. We are worshipping the true and living GOD who sees the motivation of our hearts.)*

Later, some jealous and envious people around the king informed him that there were three men whom he had appointed to high positions in the kingdom refusing to comply with his orders. Of course, this made the king furious. He sent for the three young men and confronted them with the accusations that had been made against them. The king told them that he would give them another chance to comply with orders. If when the music played, they bowed down and worshipped the statue, their lives would be spared. If not, no god would be able to save them from the fiery and flaming furnace into which they would be thrown.

Take note of their answer to the king. The three men answered that they did not need to defend themselves. They were confident that the GOD they served could deliver them. What's more, if GOD did not deliver them, HE was still *able* to do it. What faith! What confidence! What sweet assurance even in the face of danger!

The king became so enraged that he ordered the three young men executed immediately. His facial features were horribly contorted with uncontrollable rage. He insisted that the furnace be made seven times hotter than usual. The king also demanded that the soldiers bind them up and throw them fully clothed into the flaming furnace. *(I guess the soldiers did not know that they were not supposed to touch GOD'S anointed! Not even when acting upon someone's orders.)*

The soldiers who carried out the deed were burned with fire and paid immediately for their misdoings with their very lives. What the Bible tells us next was so amazing that every time I read this account it causes me to praise GOD!

The very king, who had concocted this false worship scheme, jumped up and looked into the furnace. "Then King Nebuchadnezzar leaped to his feet in amazement and asked his advisors "Weren't there three men that we tied up and threw into the fire?" They replied, "Certainly, O king." He said, *"Look! I see four men walking around in the fire, unbound and unharmed, and the fourth looks like the son of GOD."* (Verse 24-25 NKJV)

None of the men was tied up!! The three young men were walking around in fire hot enough to burn evil men to death yet they were free. When the kings ordered the young men to come out of the furnace, not only were they unharmed, their hair was not scorched and their clothes did not smell like fire. What had happened to them was miraculous and defied all natural or earthly laws.

This miracle was so profound that the king praised their GOD for rescuing them. GOD received all of the glory! The king was impressed that the young men trusted GOD so much they were willing to face imminent death. He made another royal decree forbidding any nation or race to say anything against the GOD of Shadrach, Meshach and Abednego

After the three men had passed their test, the very king that had previously ordered a torturous death for the three promoted them to an even higher position in Babylon. GOD had granted them favor with the king.

We do not know if the three young men were laughing in the furnace. We do know that the things that had them bound were loosed and they were seen walking about unharmed. They did not stay in the hot "**DRY PLACES**" very long.

In fact, the plot against them was so vile, so evil and designed to bring about such a torturous death, that GOD immediately dispatched help. This was such an unfair fight that GOD moved quickly to rescue them. Their answer in the face of danger was correct. They did not have to defend themselves because this battle belonged to the LORD.

GOD has granted us the gift of the HOLY SPIRIT to reside within us at all times. HE has promised to never leave nor to forsake us. The only way that we are left alone to deal with a problem is if we choose to do it on our own. The "**DRY PLACES**" should remind us that there are some things we cannot handle on our own. We should be totally dependent on the HOLY SPIRIT with no need to ever defend ourselves.

I once heard it said by a speaker, "I do not have problems." What an incredible claim. As soon as she got a problem, she gave it to JESUS in prayer. Once she did that, it became a JESUS problem! What a word, if we cast our cares on JESUS as soon as we get them we too will never have problems!

Scriptures promises in the fifth chapter of Job verses nineteen through twenty-two, "*You will laugh at destruction and famine, and need not fear the beasts of the earth. For you will have a covenant with the stones of the field, and the wild animals will be at peace with you. You will know that your tent is secure; you will take stock of your property and find nothing missing. You'll shrug off disaster and famine, and stroll fearlessly among wild animals.*"

Even if you are miserably crying now in the "**DRY PLACES**" remember "*. . . Blessed are you who weep now, for you will laugh.*" Luke 6:21b. NIV. GOD will deliver you and set you free!

In the book, *The Power of Obedience* by Myrtice Robinson, the author gives her personal testimony about a troublesome sleep disorder. She recounts how in the midst of her test and trials she discovered her fun time with GOD. Our LORD moved on her the thoughts and said, "*I am fun, I created fun!*"

I like that. The best fun any one of us can have is with the LORD. Laugh now as you praise your way out of the "**DRY PLACES**." You operate in the realm of the supernatural. Do not let anything or anyone keep you down in the "**DRY PLACES**." Every new situation is an opportunity to learn more about GOD. As you develop, you will find yourself growing more confident, emerging more victorious and escalating to a supernatural realm of existence. Keep looking up and laughing out loud because great is your reward with GOD!

Dear FATHER In Heaven,

I love YOU and I thank YOU for teaching me to laugh in the midst of trouble knowing that everything will work together for my good. The joy that I have in YOU does not depend on what is happening around me. I know that YOUR love for me is everlasting so I praise YOUR name. In the name of JESUS I pray,

Amen.

STOP

TAKE A

PRAISE

BREAK!

When you consider how GOD has comforted you in the past, begin to thank and praise HIM!

- ✓ *PRAISE GOD FOR THE PROMISES IN HIS WORD.*

- ✓ *PRAISE GOD FOR SUPERNATURALLY TURNING THINGS AROUND FOR YOUR GOOD!*

- ✓ *PRAISE GOD FOR GIVING YOU THE GARMENT OF PRAISE FOR THE SPIRIT OF HEAVINESS!*

CHAPTER TEN

The Passion

*"Carpe diem! Rejoice while you are alive;
enjoy the day; live life to the fullest;
make the most of what you have.
It is later than you think."*
—Horace

*"Nothing great in the world has
been accomplished without passion."*
—Georg Wilhelm

*Yesterday is but a dream,
and tomorrow is only a vision,
but today well-lived makes every
yesterday a dream of happiness
and every tomorrow a vision of hope.*
—Anonymous

I once read the account of a person who met the love of her life. She had finally met someone who seemed to have a similar outlook on life. They fell deeply in love and after a whirlwind courtship, they became engaged.

The couple immediately began planning a lavish wedding and invited both sets of families, friends and acquaintances. They decided to postpone their enjoyment until after the wedding ceremony. This couple had a lot of planning to do. The wedding was beautiful and everything they had hoped for. Still, the couple decided to delay their enjoyment because they had scheduled a two-week honeymoon cruise, through the Caribbean, aboard a brand new luxury liner. This couple wanted to make sure that they got to the port on time with their passports, beach gear and everything necessary for formal nights aboard the ship!

The exquisite appointments of the honeymoon suite was amazing with a private balcony, a butler on call and an invitation waiting for them to dine at the captain's table Once again, this couple chose to wait to enjoy themselves because when they returned they would move into a brand new dream home in a gated community!

Their first night home, friends had surprised them with a huge housewarming basket packed with all types of household goodies. In this case, the couple did not enjoy themselves because the next day the movers would arrive with their belongings. *(Some of which were brand new and purchased for the new home)*. Rather than enjoying themselves, they both were too busy being consumed with worry that everything would go off without a hitch.

You get the picture. All through life, this couple postponed their joy and was constantly obsessed with worry about the next thing. They both went to their graves never truly enjoying what was right before them. They never developed a passion for life.

Sometimes in our Christian faith, we can live a passionless life on the fringes of the "**DRY PLACES**." Nothing is wrong but nothing is right either. It is a bland, lukewarm existence bringing joy to no one. That type of life causes the "**DRY PLACES**" to appear vaster than they really are.

All around as far as the eye can see, it seems that the "**DRY PLACES**" go on and on.

If you too are a lukewarm, bland and passionless Christian, you should reexamine your initial conversion. The wonder of it all should bring about a passionate sense of awe and gratitude. Thanksgiving and praise should ring from your heart constantly. To have passion for CHRIST is to have a very strong feeling and a very strong love. It is fervent and requires an outward expression of our adoration of the risen Savior. It will cause us to put all of our heart mind and soul into loving GOD. It produces a deep-seated unspeakable joy that cannot be taken away by the cares of life.

This passionate joy provides our strength to praise our way out of the "**DRY PLACES.**" We must discover how to immerse ourselves in joy and find the way to enjoy all times in our lives if we ever hope to achieve victory outside of the "**DRY PLACES.**" Each new experience always brings new insight and greater understanding if approached with a proper outlook.

Seven early churches in the province of Asia received revelations about its conditions. A common thread ran through each of them. I noticed as I studied the Bible about passion that each church had an angel to whom John was instructed to address his letters. *(**Read Revelations 2 & 3**)*

The first angel to the church in Ephesus was written the message of assurance that GOD knew their deeds, hard work and perseverance. That church had endured hardships for the name of the LORD and had not grown weary. Yet GOD still had something against them. That church had forsaken its first love. In other words, the thrill was gone. No more passion. They were urged to repent and to redo the things they did at first.

To the second angel of the church in Smyrna, the vision given let that church know that GOD knew of its afflictions and poverty. It also confirmed that they were yet rich! They were encouraged not to be afraid of test and trials ahead. To remain faithful even to the point of death and receive the crown of life. Again, passion is needed to fuel the tenacity to never let go!

The third angel of the church in Pergamum was given the pronouncement that even in the face of the adversary they remained true to the LORD'S name. This church did not renounce its faith when others were martyred in their very city. Yet GOD still had *somewhat* against this church because they compromised their standard by tolerating sexual immorality. GOD urged them to repent immediately. They were to be passionate on every hand in their stand for the LORD.

The fourth angel for Thyatira's church was written that although their deeds of love and faith were known by GOD, there was still something held against them. In their midst were seducers who were so beguiling that they were called Jezebel. These seducers drew people away from the truth and into immorality and eating food sacrificed to idols. While this church had the reputation for improvement in their service, the very source of their passion was false. GOD gave this church the chance to stop before a judgment was unleashed upon them.

The fifth angel of the church in Sardis was written a warning about sleep walking through life. Although the church's reputation was a lively one, they were actually dead. If this church did not wake up and strengthen what remained they would miss the eternal blessing stored away for them. They were not all bad though, some in this church were equipped with the Godly passion to do what pleased GOD and they were encouraged to continue.

Written to the sixth angel of the church in Philadelphia were the assurances that GOD knew their deeds and promised to place before them an open door that no one could shut. GOD knew that they had a little strength, yet they had kept HIS word and had not denied HIS name. The LORD told that church HE was coming soon and to hold on to what they had so that no one would take its crown. This church enjoyed a passionate relationship with the LORD and was reciprocated with divine love.

Finally, to the seventh angel of the church in Laodicea it was written that GOD knew their deeds. That church was neither cold nor hot. Therefore, because they were lukewarm, neither hot nor cold, GOD would spit them out of HIS mouth! GOD loved this church enough to rebuke and discipline them. The LORD promised to knock at the door of their hearts, or give them another chance. They were given the opportunity to ignite their passion for the LORD that would remove them from a lukewarm state.

Passion brings about movement and joy. Even if you may appear to be standing still to outward observers, inside your heart may be soaring with thoughts of love and praise to GOD Almighty. The day-to-day routine of life may cause you to flirt with the notion of a sabbatical in the "**DRY PLACES**" but rouse yourself with passionate praise of the wonderful things that have already transpired in your life. Remember the act of giving HIS very life for you and me is called the passion of CHRIST. HE held nothing back but gave HIS all for us.

"Looking unto JESUS the author and finisher of our faith; who for the joy that was set before him endured the cross, despising the shame, and is set down at the right hand of the throne of GOD." Heb 12:2 KJV

At the start of this chapter, you read about the couple who was abundantly blessed yet did not take the time to enjoy their lives. Most could reason within their hearts, "If I had the opportunity to cruise the Caribbean in a luxurious suite, I'd be happy. Just the mere thought of it would keep me satisfied for years. On the other hand, if in my life I could own a brand new home, I would forever be grateful. Unfortunately, most of us are just like the couple. Our lives may appear glorious to someone else looking from the outside. Others may be able to chronicle some successes in our lives that we have not acknowledged. Greed steps in for some who always wants more money, more recognition and more prestige. *(Some will sell their souls to get it! Have mercy LORD)* Nothing for them is ever enough. Nothing ever brings about contentment.

At some point, we should grow to the point that the passion we have for CHRIST causes a deep sense of satisfaction to come into our hearts. Decide today, to enjoy your life. Be grateful, be appreciative and make up your mind to travel through the "**DRY PLACES**" merely as an observer. Trust GOD that these journeys will teach you things you never knew before. Know that you were never meant to stay forever in the "**DRY PLACES**" and that the joy in the LORD will give you the strength to make it through them. Remember that this type of joy is a passion that only GOD can give you and no one can take it away. As you passionately praise your way through, keep a smile on your face, a song on your lips and joy in your heart!

Heavenly FATHER,

*I passionately love YOU and thank YOU
for YOUR many blessings in my life.
I know that it pleases YOU to see me
enjoy my life. I know YOU delight
in my getting closer to YOU
each day through my prayer life.
I commit today to praise YOU in every
situation and through all circumstances.
I speak joy and contentment
in every area of my life.
In JESUS' name, I pray.*

Amen.

ELEVEN

The Peace

"O LORD, make me an instrument of Thy Peace!
Where there is hatred, let me sow love.
Where there is injury, pardon.
Where there is discord, harmony.
Where there is doubt, faith.
Where there is despair, hope.
Where there is darkness, light.
Where there is sorrow, joy.

Oh Divine Master, grant that I may not
so much seek to be consoled as to console;
to be understood as to understand;
to be loved as to love;
for it is in giving that we receive;
it is in pardoning that we are pardoned;
and it is in dying that we are born to Eternal Life."

The exact origin of this beautiful prayer remains unknown; it does not appear in any known writings of St Francis. The first known appearance of this inspiring prayer was in 1912 when it was published in the French magazine La Clochette.
—Saint Francis of Assisi, The Peace Prayer of Saint Francis
(often referred to as "The Prayer of Saint Francis of

What happens when you receive bad news about your loved ones? Maybe someone has gotten a disturbing report from a doctor's appointment. Maybe surgery is imminent with a lengthy recuperation. Perhaps you were told shocking news so perplexing that you are between a rock and a hard place within one of the "**DRY PLACES!**" How can you get yourself out of there?

For several months, I wore a silver band with the words peace inscribed on it. The inexpensive trinket that was purchased at a Bible bookstore has become invaluable to me. Many things happened during the months that I wore this simple ring. Hospital visits were made to seriously ill church members who were frightened and looking for comfort. Numerous members called upon me for counsel as they confronted perplexing problems. Many had to deal with disappointment, hurt, anger and emptiness.

I was called upon to serve at funerals, to preach eulogies and share words of comfort at gravesite committals. Even my personal life had astonished me with career setbacks and a bout of poor health. Fear was rapidly engulfing everything in life. What in the world was going on!

It was then that GOD began to teach me about peace. GOD given peace is an intangible tangible that covers you like a blanket. Peace soothes your soul and brings an absolute calmness to your heart. It is freedom from strife of any kind and a deep sense of security.

Peace of mind allows you to move through the "**DRY PLACES**' in confidence. Not in torment and worry about what the next day will bring. Not hurting about difficulties in relationships or misunderstandings that might arise. Rather, you can serenely face every new challenge.

Peace is one of the fruits of the spirit and is a by-product of living a life for CHRIST. It has no room for petty jealousies and grudges. In my last book, ***Help To Get Over It,*** we discussed biblical solutions for dealing with grudges. We even considered grudges that someone holds against you. As ugly as this situation can be, our part is to remain peaceable and to refuse to take part in sending and receiving grudges. It was likened unto getting a dirty, nasty, smelly and despicable package sent special delivery to our front doors. It is our choice! We can open our doors and allow that vile package to defile our beautiful home or we can refuse to receive it and return it to the sender unopened!

Peace will help us to focus our attention on the lovely and pure things in life rather than reacting rashly to negativity. Peace will allow us to be patient with the spiritually immature and to continue to walk in love towards them as they begin to grow in grace. Peace calls for *p*ersistently *e*ncountering *a*wkward *c*ircumstances *e*ffortlessly!

In the fourth chapter of Mark, we read where JESUS was teaching one day before such a large crowd, that HE entered a boat and taught beside Lake Galilee. HE taught the parable about the farmer scattering seed and mustard seed faith. JESUS also explained to the disciples why HE taught in parables. They were fortunate to be a part of the inner circle of CHRIST because HE gave the interpretations. When JESUS finished teaching, HE told the disciples to take the boat to the other side and HE lay down to get some sleep.

Suddenly a windstorm struck the lake. Picture violent waves thrashing about and hear the sounds the wind made. Among the disciples in the boat were seasoned fishermen who no doubt had experienced windstorms before. This storm however, was so violent that water entered the boat filling it to the point that the disciples thought that they would all die.

They went down in the boat and woke JESUS up! The disciples were so panicked that they asked JESUS if HE cared that they were about to die. I love what JESUS said to the wind and the waves; "Peace! Be still!" Those three words caused the wind to cease and there was great calm.

Then JESUS dealt with the disciples. After all, they had seen and experienced that day HE asked them, "Why are you afraid? Have you no faith?" Can it be that some of us are like the disciples with no faith? It is difficult to have peace without faith and faith without peace. It is impossible to please GOD without faith. It then follows that somehow faith and peace going together pleases GOD.

JESUS knew that as humans, we could fall apart easily at times. Men and women do it as well as the young and old. For that reason, HE decided in the twentieth chapter of John to leave this reassurance, Again JESUS said,

"Peace be with you! As the FATHER has sent me, I am sending you." And with that, HE breathed on them and said, "Receive the HOLY SPIRIT.

The HOLY SPIRIT is essential to peace for governing our lives. JESUS knew that it would take Godly peace to remain focused enough to accomplish the things that GOD has purposed for us. We have been sent unto the world as a witness of the love of JESUS. We have to let our lights shine before men and women and share the good news so that other souls will be won to the kingdom.

We have also been called to strive for peace, to follow peace and to be the peacemakers even when we did not break the peace. Some times a soft word, an apology or the validation of someone else's feelings when they are upset is all it takes to restore peace. In making peace it does not mean being spineless to avoid strife. Particularly in relationships, this type of evasion lacks integrity and temporarily dodges sincere confrontation. By evading the issue, people in the conflict lose the opportunity to work toward a solution that will bring about genuine peace.

If there is genuine or true peace, it leads us to conclude that the can be false peace. Usually, false peace comes from unscrupulous people and is designed to deceive. That is the beauty of peace however. GOD grants discernment through the HOLY SPIRIT and if your motives are pure, GOD gives you peace of mind and the other party owns all of the ill feelings. You are no longer held responsible.

It will also take peace when we reach crossroads in our lives to decide which directions to take. Where there is peace there is love. Where there is love, there is no fear. Without fear, decisions can be made by confidently seeking GOD in prayer trusting that the outcome will be fine. Peace allows us to know that no good thing will GOD withhold from us because we walk uprightly before HIM. Sometimes we may need to seek Godly and wise counsel from others to solve dilemmas. Peace allows us to admit to ourselves when we need help. We no longer feel the need to pretend self-sufficiency.

Peace with GOD and others helps us when we face betrayal from those we would have never suspected. Betrayal by definition can only occur with someone close to us. As painful as it may seem, peace sends serenity to cloak us with the assurance that whatever was meant for evil against us, GOD supernaturally turns around for our good.

Peace will also cause us to see GOD when others reject us, overlook us and mistreat us. GOD will honor us, protect us and grant us unspeakable joy.

Our FATHER, JEHOVAH-SHALOM is the very essence of peace. As children of GOD, this attribute passes unto us like a family trait. It is an essential element in the spiritual kingdom of GOD. It is soundness, well being and is often translated as prosperity. We never have to suffer from a bad day nor be held captive in the **"DRY PLACES"** if we choose to meditate on the Holy Word each day and allow the peace it brings to reside within us.

Remember the wonderful promises reserved for those who believe. GOD promised to never leave us or forsake us. GOD promised that the Messiah would come. GOD promised the gift of eternal life. GOD promised to blot out our wrongdoing. GOD promised to forget our sins and GOD promised perfect peace if we keep our minds on HIM.

The peace that surpasses all understanding surrounds and protects us. It covers us with visible serenity that allows us to calmly and confidently praise GOD. It transforms the **"DRY PLACES"** into a lush fertile oasis and allows us to coolly travel out!

Dear LORD,

*I Love YOU. Thank YOU for
covering me with YOUR peace.
Help me to be a peacemaker and
to live in peace with others around me.
Thank YOU for teaching me that to have peace
is to have prosperity. I will continue to exalt YOU
each day of my life. Anywhere there is strife and confusion,
I speak peace. I set free the fruits of love, joy, peace,
patience, kindness, goodness, faithfulness,
gentleness and self-control.
In the name of JESUS, I pray,*

Amen.

CHAPTER TWELVE

The Favor

Fortune favors the brave.
—Terence (BC 195-159)

"Heaven goes by favor..."
—Mark Twain (1835-1910)

"I believe that favor is the greatest harvest that you could ever receive from GOD. Favor is better than money."
—Dave Martin, Author

We have come to the end of our journeys through many of the **"DRY PLACES."** We know that twist and turns in life can suddenly propel us to these spots. We also know that we can languish within them indefinitely until we become dried up and unfruitful people. We have a choice to pick ourselves up and keep moving, or remain stuck in desert places allowing the scavengers to pick our flesh clean. As my daughter states, we all have two choices in all situations to stay or to step. GOD will help us make the choice when we must stay or when it is necessary to step. HE will always send help and the resources we need to prosper along the way.

GOD grants us FAVOR which is good will and kindness running over and flowing with benefits to us. This FAVOR provides our acceptance in the Beloved and gives us grace. It causes people to do nice things for us just to be helpful. Many times FAVOR comes in unexpected ways.

Have you ever driven to a very crowded shopping mall packed with row after row of parked cars? Just as you round the corner to head towards the back row, someone pulls out and you are able to park your car right up front! That is FAVOR.

Perhaps you have been shopping during the busy holiday season. While at the check out counter, you may have laid your wallet down as you paid for your purchases. As you rush out of the store, someone calls from behind you, "You left your wallet!" After you thank the person and check your wallet, you realize that nothing is missing! Again, that is FAVOR.

Maybe you have nursed a secret desire for an item of clothing, a particular outing or a special gadget. Just maybe someone surprises you with the very thing you had secretly hoped for at a time that you most needed encouragement! Thank GOD for FAVOR.

In every instance, we should thank the LORD for HIS FAVOR, acts of kindness and unexpected blessings! Often when we are in the **"DRY PLACES"**, we can forget to be thankful that things are as well as they are. It is another trick of the enemy to cause us to miss the many acts of FAVOR that happen in our lives everyday.

I tell you, now is the time of GOD'S favor, now is the day of salvation. 2 Corinthians 6:2 NIV

FAVOR is GOD'S friendship and fellowship. FAVOR gives fearless focus for GOD'S direction and leading for our lives. Yea, though we may walk through the valley of the shadow of death, we will fear no evil!

FAVOR brings abundance, anointing and GOD'S authority to our lives. Favor grants us the ability to accomplish all that GOD has assigned for us.

With FAVOR, we are not unduly influenced by occurrences, perceptions and incidents around us. We remain confident that GOD who began a good work in us will see it through to completion. Even when experiencing difficult days, GOD'S FAVOR assures victorious outcomes and overflow blessings. FAVOR allows us to enjoy sweet rest as we relax in very center of GOD'S will for us. With FAVOR, we know that when we belong to GOD people will go out of their way to help us!

One of the most memorable stories about favor is the story of Queen Esther. She was a beautiful Jewish maiden who had been summoned to the royal court to replace Queen Vashti.

After Queen Vashti had presumptuously disgraced herself, the king had decreed that young virgins be brought to the royal palace so that a replacement could be selected. This was the very first opportunity for FAVOR in Esther's life because she was an orphan girl of lowly birth and an unpopular nationality.

"When the king's order and edict had been proclaimed, many girls were brought to the citadel of Susa and put under the care of Hegai. Esther also was taken to the king's palace and entrusted to Hegai, who had charge of the harem. The girl pleased him and won his favor. Immediately he provided her with her beauty treatments and special food. He assigned to her seven maids selected from the king's palace and moved her and her maids into the best place in the harem." Esther 2:8-9 NIV

Before a girl could be presented to the king for consideration, she had to complete twelve months of beauty treatments. The wonderful lesson we learn about Esther at this point is that she submitted to the rigorous treatments. When it was her turn to be presented to the king, she listened to instructions and selected what was recommended.

"When the turn came for Esther (the girl Mordecai had adopted, the daughter of his uncle Abihail) to go to the king, she asked for nothing other than what Hegai, the king's eunuch who was in charge of the harem, suggested. And Esther won the favor of everyone who saw her." Esther 2:15 NIV

The Bible informs us that the king was attracted to Esther more than to any of the other women. She had won his FAVOR so he set a royal crown on her head and made her queen instead of Vashti. The king was so pleased that he gave a banquet for all his nobles and officials. He proclaimed a holiday throughout the provinces and distributed gifts with royal liberality.

FAVOR can cause a disagreeable person to become a pleasure to be around. One of the by products of FAVOR is generosity. When FAVOR is at work, it makes others happy to be in the reflected glory.

After winning this coveted elevation as Queen, Esther remained a dutiful niece to the uncle who had raised her. One day she discovered that her uncle sat sorrowfully outside the palace in sackcloths. During that time this behavior could mean instant death if discovered by the king.

When Esther found out about her uncle, she was deeply distressed and sent clothing to him to replace the sackcloth, but he refused to wear them. Esther then sent for one of the king's eunuchs who had been appointed as her attendant, to find out what was troubling him.

An evil plot had been hatched to annihilate her entire nation of people, as Esther's nationality was not yet known in the palace. A certain day had been set aside to put to death every Jewish person within the region. The culprit had pledged to pay almost 10,000 talents of silver into the king's treasury for the destruction of the Jewish people. (Esther 3:9 NASB)

Initially Esther was fearful to intercede on behalf of her people. It was the custom to never appear before the king unless summoned. If a person dared to show up uninvited, the king could extend his royal scepter granting life. Otherwise, the poor unlucky person would be executed on the spot.

Her uncle had to persuade her to consider if she was in the perfect place at the right time for this occasion to offer help. She had influence with the king who was thought to be the only person capable of turning the decree around. If her assistance was refused though, Esther could still lose her life.

Esther asked her uncle to gather all of the Jewish people together that they may fast for her. She agreed to do the same for three days and three nights. At the end of that time, she would go to the king. Esther declared, *"If I perish, I perish: but I'm going to see the king!"* (Verse 16)

What a bold conviction. Esther knew she needed supernatural intervention and FAVOR. She appealed to someone higher than an earthly king and someone far greater.

Three days later Esther put on her royal robes and entered the inner court where the king was sitting upon his royal throne. Once the king saw Esther, he welcomed her and held out the golden scepter. He asked her what she wanted. He promised to give it to her even if it was half the kingdom.

Esther was wise with her request. She asked that the king come to a banquet she had prepared for him. She asked that he bring her mortal enemy, as well without yet revealing that he was the source of her displeasure. Notice that the banquet was already prepared when she extended the invitation. Notice also that Esther knew how to bide her time.

While at the banquet during the wine course, the king asked Esther again what she really wanted. She did not reply, "Off with the head of my enemy!" instead, she invited them both to a banquet on the next day. She promised to explain what it was all about on the next day.

That very night the king had trouble sleeping and decided to read. He read the historical records of his kingdom and came across the item telling how Esther's uncle exposed an assassination plot by two of the king's guards. The king discovered that he had done nothing to reward Esther's uncle.

What irony, the very culprit that had plotted against Esther and her people was the one who was ordered by the king to put royal robes on her uncle.

Esther's enemy was the one who had to arrange for Esther's uncle to be paraded through the street with a royal crown on the king's own horse and the proclamation, "This is the way the king honors those who truly please him!"

When the king along with the culprit went to Esther's banquet later that day, he again asked for her petition.

Finally, Queen Esther replied, *"If I have won your favor, O king, and if it pleases Your Majesty, save my life and the lives of my people. For I and my people have been sold to those who will destroy us. We are doomed to destruction and slaughter."* (Esther 7: 3-4 TLB)

The king became furious. He could not believe that someone would dare touch his wife. It is very foolish and very dangerous to try to harm the wife of the king. The king demanded to know who would do such a thing. When Esther revealed her wicked enemy as Haman, the king jumped to his feet and went out into the palace garden as Haman, the culprit, stood up to plead for his life. In despair, Haman fell upon the couch where Queen Esther was reclining, just as the king returned from the palace garden.

This did not bode well with the king. It appeared that Haman was trying to molest the queen. The king roared and instantly the death veil was placed over Haman's face. Haman was killed by the very gallows he constructed to destroy another!

With FAVOR, Queen Esther was able to save her life and those of her people. She was prepared to die if necessary, but still used wisdom to woo the king. With the close relationship she enjoyed with the king, she was able to influence a life altering change.

Never forget that a stay in any of the "**DRY PLACES**" could be fatal to you, your family and to your ministry. You were not designed for the "**DRY PLACES**." GOD has something better for you. You are blessed and highly favored! Do not give up. Do not dry out. Do not wither away. Let GOD'S HOLY SPIRIT refresh you. Keep growing and keep going!

Your growth will produce the following actions of:

- Praying & Waiting.
- Letting Go & Forgiving.
- Confidently relying on GOD'S Provision.
- Leading & Serving by the HOLY SPIRIT.
- Living in Peace and Giving Thanks.
- Being content in GOD'S FAVOR.

Begin to praise GOD just because HE is GOD and say bye-bye to the ***"DRY PLACES!"***

"That is what is meant by the Scriptures which say that no mere man has ever seen, heard, or even imagined what wonderful things GOD has ready for those who love the LORD. But we know about these things because GOD has sent his Spirit to tell us, and his Spirit searches out and shows us all of GOD'S deepest secrets." 1Corinthians 2:9-10 TLB

Dear Heavenly FATHER,

*Thank YOU for the favor YOU have
placed upon my life. Thank YOU for sending
YOUR precious HOLY SPIRIT to help me through
the fatally "DRY PLACES" that will try to keep me
from living the wonderful life YOU have planned for me.
Thank YOU for being Elohim,
My Creator; El Roi, The GOD Who Sees;
Jehovah-jireh, my provider; Jehovah-rapha,
my healer; Jehovah-nissi, my banner;
Jehovah-shalom my peace and
Jehovah-rohi, my shepherd.
For the rest of my life I promise
to serve YOU, LORD.
In the name of JESUS, I pray.*

Amen.

Your Personal Growth Declaration

I will Bless *YOU, LORD* at all times *YOUR* praise shall continually be in my mouth. I love *YOU LORD*, with all that is within me! No good thing will *YOU* withhold from me as I walk uprightly before *YOU*. *YOU* oh *GOD* will supply all my need according to *YOUR* riches in glory. *YOU* will not in any degree leave me helpless nor forsake me nor relax *YOUR* hold on me! No weapon formed against me will ever be able to prosper. There is nothing that I face in my life that is too big for YOU to handle. *YOUR* will for me is physical, emotional and spiritual health. *YOUR* Holy Word declares that it is *YOUR* will for me to prosper and be in health as my soul prospers. My mouth is full of laughter and my tongue with singing. When I humble myself under *YOUR* mighty hand, *YOU* will exalt me in due time. *YOUR* FAVOR refreshes me now. It restores me and gives back all of the JOY the enemy had stolen. *YOUR* FAVOR rejuvenates me and lifts me to a "Brand New" place in *YOU*. I eagerly embrace my future with confidence knowing that *YOU* have begun a good work in me and will complete it. I *commit to YOU, LORD* everything I do so that my plans will succeed!

STOP

TAKE A
PRAISE
BREAK!

When you consider everything GOD has done for you up to this point in your life begin to thank and praise HIM!

- ✓ *PRAISE GOD FOR GRANTING YOU PERFECT PEACE!*

- ✓ *PRAISE GOD FOR FAVOR!*

- ✓ *PRAISE GOD FOR A BRAND NEW START!*

ABOUT THE AUTHOR

Diana Rose Williams

D. R. WILLIAMS lives with her husband JOHN M. WILLIAMS in the Atlanta, Georgia area. She is the mother of four daughters and one son, two sons-in-law, one daughter-in-law and has three *Nana* babies. Diana R. Williams is an ordained Minister, published author and dynamic inspirational coach with over twenty years of ministry expertise.

Called GOD'S *Cheerleader*, she has a passion for sharing with others about the love of GOD through writing, preaching and teaching HIS precepts. D. R. Williams is a prolific writer with a special gift for making the Bible plain so that most men and women can easily grasp its meaning and apply it to their lives.

She has written numerous uplifting, and stimulating articles, Bible studies and daily devotions. The LORD has inspired Diana Williams to develop a refreshing web ministry *www.DianaWilliams.org* to spread hope and encouragement in CHRIST JESUS around the world. She speaks at retreats, symposiums, conferences, seminars and themed events for churches, colleges, civic groups, social clubs and family organizations geared to boost morale and inspire each attendee to passionately embrace his or her future. Her exciting and powerful messages include topics of adversity, change, family issues, leadership, personal empowerment, spirituality and religion, team building, vision and women issues. Her slogan, inspired by Habakkuk 2:2, is" *Plainly Writing and Telling the Vision!*"

Order Page

This book is the second in the HELP! (Hope, Empowerment, Love, Prayer) Series. Often, life can cause many people to feel less than inspired and optimistic about the future. Whenever there have been disappointing incidents, bouts of disillusionment and periods of difficulty, people can find themselves in the "DRY PLACES". Like the first book; Help To GET OVER IT, these chapters expound on biblical accounts that will offer help for the readers. The "DRY PLACES" are passionless and gloomy locations constructed to rob its occupants of the power and joy of the HOLY SPIRIT. Share your insights, request prayer, or add your name to the HELP! Mailing list by contacting the author.

www.dianawilliams.org

BVG